Better Homes and Gardens.

WOOD.

TURNING TECHNIQUES

AND PROJECTS YOU CAN MAKE

WECARE!

All of us at Meredith® Books are dedicated to giving you the
information and ideas you need to create beautiful and useful
woodworking projects. We guarantee your satisfaction with this
book for as long as you own it. We also welcome your comments
and suggestions. Please write us at Meredith® Books, RW-240,
1716 Locust St., Des Moines, IA 50309-3023.

A **WOOD** BOOK
Published by Meredith® Books

MEREDITH® BOOKS
President, Book Group: Joseph J. Ward
Vice President and Editorial Director: Elizabeth P. Rice
Executive Editor: Connie Schrader
Art Director: Ernest Shelton
Prepress Production Manager: Randall Yontz

WOOD® MAGAZINE
President, Magazine Group: William T. Kerr
Editor: Larry Clayton

TURNING TECHNIQUES AND PROJECTS YOU CAN MAKE
Produced by Roundtable Press, Inc.
Directors: Susan E. Meyer, Marsha Melnick
Senior Editor: Marisa Bulzone
Managing Editor: Ross L. Horowitz
Graphic Designer: Leah Lococo
Design Assistant: Leslie Goldman
Art Assistant: Ahmad Mallah
Copy Assistant: Amy Handy

For Meredith® Books
Editorial Project Manager/Assistant Art Director: Tom Wegner
Contributing How-To Editors: Marlen Kemmet,
    Charles E. Sommers
Contributing Techniques Editor: Bill Krier
Contributing Tool Editor: Larry Johnston
Contributing Outline Editor: David A. Kirchner

Special thanks to Khristy Benoit

Meredith Corporation Corporate Officers:
Chairman of the Executive Committee: E. T. Meredith III
Chairman of the Board, President and Chief Executive Officer:
    Jack D. Rehm
Group Presidents: Joseph J. Ward, Books; William T. Kerr, Magazines;
    Philip A. Jones, Broadcasting; Allen L. Sabbag, Real Estate
Vice Presidents: Leo R. Armatis, Corporate Relations;
    Thomas G. Fisher, General Counsel and Secretary;
    Larry D. Hartsook, Finance; Michael A. Sell, Treasurer;
    Kathleen J. Zehr, Controller and Assistant Secretary

TURNING JIGS AND TOOLS

The right tools make the difference in any turning project. Here are tips on buying and caring for your turning tools—and make-your-own equipment that will add a professional touch to work produced in any home shop.

TURNING JIG FOR BETTER BOTTOMS

When people stop to admire your plates or bowls, do they peek at the bottoms to see if you've left any tell-tale screw holes? If so, then add this jig to your turning arsenal, and you'll be able to turn bottoms as well as the pros.

1. The jig shown here was built to fit our lathe, which has a 7½" swing (distance from the center of the headstock spindle to the bed). The outside diameter of the jig you build will depend on your particular lathe. Provide at least ½" clearance between the jig and bed. The diameter of the opening in the collar and the length of the machine screws will vary depending on the size of your turnings. We use several collars, all with different-size openings.

2. After attaching a 6"-diameter auxiliary faceplate and a large disc to your 6" metal faceplate, start the lathe and use a scraper to true up the outside face of the large disc. The outside disc always seems to have a little wobble.

3. Start the lathe again, and use a pencil or felt-tipped marker to mark concentric circles on the face of the large wood disc about ½" apart. These circles will make it easier when centering turnings on the disc later. Using an outside calipers, measure the thickness of the bowl bottom. This will come in handy when turning the bottom to shape, so you don't turn too deep and go through the base.

4. Mount your plate or bowl, bottom side out, where shown in the Section View drawing. Use mounting screws that stick out the back side of the large disc by only ¼" or ½". Tighten the three mounting screws, turn the lathe on, and observe the rotating bottom. Chances are you'll have to stop the lathe, loosen the screws slightly, adjust the turning's position, and retighten the screws. Repeat this process until the turning is perfectly centered (it always takes us about three or four tries). Turn the bottom to shape.

Project Tool List
Bandsaw
Scrollsaw or jigsaw
Lathe
    Square-end scraper
Drill press or portable drill
    ⁵⁄₁₆" bit
Router
    ⅜" round-over bit

Note: We built the project using the tools listed. You may be able to substitute other tools or equipment for listed items you don't have. Additional common hand tools and clamps may be required to complete the project.

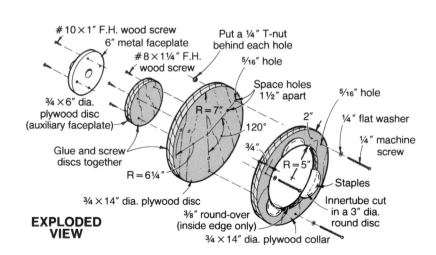

SECTION VIEW

EXPLODED VIEW

#10 × 1" F.H. wood screw
6" metal faceplate
#8 × 1¼" F.H. wood screw
¾ × 6" dia. plywood disc (auxiliary faceplate)
Glue and screw discs together
R = 6¼"
¾ × 14" dia. plywood disc
Put a ¼" T-nut behind each hole
⁵⁄₁₆" hole
Space holes 1½" apart
R = 7"
120°
¾"
⅜" round-over (inside edge only)
¾ × 14" dia. plywood collar
⁵⁄₁₆" hole
2"
¼" flat washer
¼" machine screw
R = 5"
Staples
Innertube cut in a 3" dia. round disc

CONSTRUCT-A-CHUCK

Equipping a high-school wood shop on a limited budget can be tough. And, buying lathe chucks, often costing as much as $200, is almost out of the question. To solve this problem, Dave Hout, an industrial arts teacher at Coventry High School in Akron, Ohio, decided to make his own chuck.

Note: To prevent the completed chuck from distorting after turning it to final shape, select a piece of kiln-dried, dense hardwood such as cherry or maple.

For added holding strength in securing the wood chuck to the metal faceplate, you may want to drill three additional mounting screws through the 3" faceplate and into the chuck. Then, secure with an additional three screws.

And finally, to ensure that the faceplate remains centered on the chuck, Dave recommends leaving the chuck permanently attached to the metal faceplate.

Here's how to make your hardwood chuck

1. To make the chuck, you'll need a 3½"-square laminated or solid hardwood block that measures 4" long. Crosscut the ends of the block square. Draw diagonals from corner to corner on each end of the block, and mount it between centers on your lathe.

2. At a speed of about 800 rpm, turn the block round to a diameter of 3⅜" (we used a ½" gouge). Using a parting tool, turn the tailstock end flat (square to the cylinder) where shown on Drawing A *opposite*.

3. Remove the cylinder from the lathe, and chisel off the nub. Center and fasten the squared end to a 3" faceplate (we used 1" sheet metal screws).

4. Mount the faceplate/cylinder assembly to the headstock. Start the lathe and turn the cylinder to a 3¼" diameter. Turn the tailstock end flat for a 3" finished length.

5. Using the dimensions on the full-sized End View drawing, pencil in the locations of the two recesses. Then, with a parting tool, turn the recesses ⅝"-deep in the end of the cylinder as shown in Drawing B *opposite*. When making the final cuts to form the ⅛"-thick inner-jaw wall, hold the parting tool square to the end of the cylinder. For a secure grip on turning projects later, the inner-jaw wall must be perpendicular to the end of the cylinder.

6. Remove the faceplate/chuck assembly from the lathe, and clamp

it into a woodworker's vise as shown in Drawing C. Use a backsaw to cut three ⅝"-deep kerfs at 60-degree intervals through the center of the chuck's end where shown on the End View drawing.

7. Remove a 1"-long section in the outer wall for later access to the hose-clamp adjustment nut. (To do this, we securely fastened the assembly in a large handscrew clamp, chucked a ⅝" Forstner bit into our drill press, and drilled away 1" of the ⅛" outer wall on one side of a kerf. Then, clean the drilled edge with a chisel.)

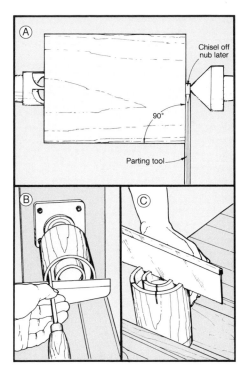

8. For ease in removing turnings from the chuck later with a knock-out bar, drill a hole through the center of your faceplate and through the center of the chuck. A knockout bar allows you to push the turning out of the chuck. Trying to pull or twist a project out of the chuck may cause the turning to break. (Our knockout bar measures ⅜" in diameter, so we drilled a ⁷⁄₁₆" hole.)

Tips on how to use your chuck

1. Mount your workpiece between centers, and turn a 1½"-diameter tenon ⅜" to ½" long to fit *snugly* in the chuck. Stop the lathe frequently to check the fit of the tenon in the recess. Square the surface of the workpiece that fits against the end of the chuck. *Optimum grip is obtained with a tight fit of the tenon in the chuck and flush mating surfaces.*

2. Next, slip on a #28 hose clamp. Insert the tenoned end of the work-

piece into the interior recess. Now, with a screwdriver or hexagonal nut driver, tighten the hose clamp to secure the workpiece. To prevent the turning from coming out of the chuck, take light cuts with your turning tool. As with any chuck, taking large cuts or pressing too hard with a scraper can dislodge the turning from the chuck.

Project Tool List
Lathe
    Faceplate
    ½" spindle gouge
    Parting tool
Drill press
    Bits: ⅜" Forstner, ⁷⁄₁₆"

Note: We built the project using the tools listed. You may be able to substitute other tools or equipment for listed items you don't have. Additional common hand tools and clamps may be required to complete the project.

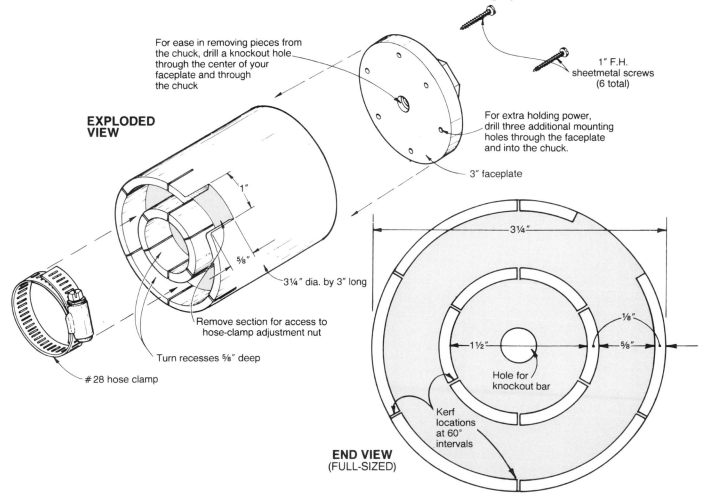

For ease in removing pieces from the chuck, drill a knockout hole through the center of your faceplate and through the chuck

1" F.H. sheetmetal screws (6 total)

EXPLODED VIEW

For extra holding power, drill three additional mounting holes through the faceplate and into the chuck.

3" faceplate

1"

5⁄8"

3¼" dia. by 3" long

Remove section for access to hose-clamp adjustment nut

Turn recesses 5⁄8" deep

#28 hose clamp

3¼"

1⁄8"

1½"

5⁄8"

Hole for knockout bar

Kerf locations at 60° intervals

END VIEW
(FULL-SIZED)

TURNING TOOLS: WHAT TO KNOW BEFORE YOU BUY

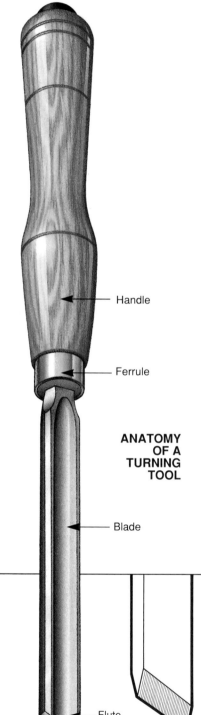

Handle

Ferrule

ANATOMY OF A TURNING TOOL

Blade

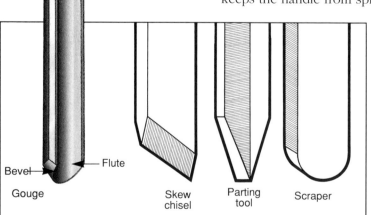

Bevel — Flute

Gouge   Skew chisel   Parting tool   Scraper

Scrapers and cutters, carbon steel, high-speed steel, bevels and flutes—today's array of turning tools seems to offer more choices than you can shake a skew at! Which of these tools does a beginning turner really need? Actually, once you learn turning tool terminology and understand just what each tool does, you can easily assemble a basic starter set for less than $100. So before you spend a bundle on tools you might not need, study the guidelines in this article. We've also included our suggestions for a starter set you can round out as your turning skills develop.

Check our illustration at *left* and you'll see that a turning tool has four or five elements, depending on the job it does. All tools consist of either flat or round steel bar stock, with a beveled *blade* at one end and a *handle* at the other. The bevel or bevels (some tools have more than one) form the edge that does the cutting. Besides being beveled, tools known as gouges are also *fluted* with a concave center that helps throw off shavings.

The other end of the tool has a wood handle, with a *ferrule* that keeps the handle from splitting.

Some tool makers offer tools without handles (though you can buy them separately) because some experienced turners prefer to turn their own. Ferrules usually are brass or steel. Steel is somewhat stronger, but the choice here is basically decorative.

The big four turning tool types

Though they come in many sizes, with lots of variations, turning tools fall into just four different classifications, illustrated *lower left*. Each type does best at a particular task, and some do several jobs well. Let's summarize their principal use:

Gouges are fluted workhorses that remove lots of material in a hurry, such as when you shape square stock into a cylinder or remove material from the inside of a bowl.

Skew chisels—so-called because the bevel is skewed at a 20–25° angle to the side of the blade—do general shaping and finish cutting on spindle turning and on the outside surfaces of faceplate projects.

Parting tools make narrow recesses or grooves. The tool gets its name because you can also use it to cut all the way through the stock, leaving it in two "parts."

Scrapers have a very shallow bevel and come in a wide variety of shapes. The flat bevel sets scrapers apart from the other three types of turning tools, because scrapers perform an entirely different role. To determine how many scrapers you should buy—if any—you need to know just what scraping tools can and can't do.

Scraping tools and cutting tools—what's the difference?

What exactly happens when you press a turning tool into a spinning piece of wood? Depending on the tool you choose and the angle at which you hold it, you'll either *cut* the wood or you'll *scrape* it.

To cut (also known as shearing), you hold the tool at an angle to the rotating stock, fairly high above its centerline, with the handle slightly down, as shown in the drawing *below*. The tool's edge—beveled 25 to 45° from the end of the blade—shears away wood. You'll know you're cutting properly when curly shavings begin to pile up on the bed of your lathe.

To scrape, you hold the tool almost perpendicular to the stock, with the handle always slightly *up*, as shown in the drawing at *bottom*.

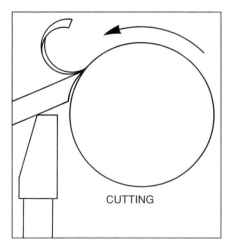

CUTTING

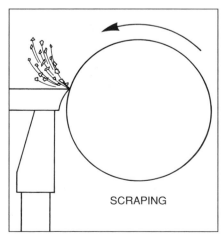

SCRAPING

Rather than shearing the wood, scraping wears it away, making dust, not shavings. Tools designed strictly for scraping have shallower, 15–20° bevels and a burr purposely left on after the edge is ground to provide the abrasion.

If you use it in the way just described, any cutting tool will also scrape, but because of the shallow bevel and burr, scrapers won't cut. So why buy scrapers at all? Actually, if your lathe work will be limited to turning between centers, you needn't invest in scrapers. If, however, you'd like to try your hand at faceplate turning, you'll find that scrapers are much better than cutters for some tasks, such as removing ridges from surfaces and finishing the inside bottom of a bowl where a gouge can't make a clean cut.

Many beginning turners start out by scraping their first projects, regardless of whether they're using a cutting or a scraping tool. Though easier than cutting, scraping takes more time and leaves a rougher surface that requires lots of sanding. We strongly recommend that you tip a cutting tool's handle down right from the start and master the cutting technique. Once you learn how to cut, quality turnings take shape in a hurry.

Tool steel—today, you have several options

As if you don't already have enough decisions to make about which turning tools to buy, manufacturers also offer a choice of tool steels. Once again, you have four options:

Carbon steel was the norm for years, and it costs the least. It also comes in the widest variety of shapes and sizes. You can quickly sharpen carbon steel, but it dulls more readily than other steels,

turning blue in the process. Careless grinding—something we are all occasionally prone to—can also cause "bluing" and ruin the edge.

High-speed steel (HSS) holds an edge much longer than carbon steel, even at the 1,000-degree-plus temperatures generated by turning. However, HSS costs about a third more than carbon steel.

Laminated steel tools utilize a forging process that bonds an extremely hard high-carbon steel cutting edge to a softer, more resilient steel backing. The result is a tool that holds a cutting edge almost as long as HSS, and can be honed to a much sharper edge. Laminated steel tools cost about twice as much as HSS versions and don't come in as wide a range of sizes and types.

For a starter set, we feel you're best off sticking with either carbon steel or HSS.

"Long and strong" vs. standard-sized tools

Standard tools all have 6" to 7" blades with 10" handles. These are big enough to handle most cutting needs, but don't try to extend the blade of a standard tool more than 4" beyond the tool rest. This puts a great deal of stress on the blade and handle, and could damage the tool or, worse yet, tear it out of your hands.

Some jobs, such as faceplate turning when you need to reach more than 4" deep into a bowl or vase, require a tool that has more length and heft than standard versions, so manufacturers have developed "long and strong" tools that are just that. Long and strong tools typically have 12" to 17" handles; the steel in these tools is longer, thicker, and wider than standard tool blades. Long and strong

continued

TURNING TOOLS: WHAT TO KNOW BEFORE YOU BUY
continued

tools offer lots of rigidity and control for big projects, especially when you're turning green wood, but their size doesn't permit detail work.

Speaking of detail work, you can also buy miniature tools that are about 8" long for small jobs.

The cost of fine turning

Sets of six or eight carbon steel tools usually cost $75 to $150; individual tools run $15–$40. As noted earlier, HSS adds about a third to the price tag of a carbon steel tool or set. Laminated steel tools come at a premium: $40 to $50 each. For long and strong tools, expect to pay $15 to $50 apiece for

them, or about $150 for a set of six. Miniatures run $10 to $20 each, about $80 for a set of eight.

Should you buy a set or individual tools?

As we've noted, some companies offer sets of up to eight turning tools. These come with matching handles and are often packaged in a handsome box. Do sets make sense for a beginning turner?

On the plus side, sets can save you 10 to 15 percent over the cost of buying the tools individually, and most sets include at least one size of all of the "big four" types listed earlier.

Trouble is, depending on the turning jobs you want to do, the set may include some tools you'll never use, and lack others you need. This particularly applies if you're mainly interested in faceplate turning. Most sets consist of nothing but spindle turning tools, though a few manufacturers have put together sets for bowl turners, too.

Whether you elect to invest in a set or buy individual tools, we think your first purchases should include the turning tools shown and discussed in the chart *below*.

WOOD® picks the basic starter set

With just six lathe turning tools you can handle most spindle work. Add a bowl gouge and a scraper or two and you can turn bowls as well. Make the tools shown here the first you buy. As your skills improve you'll undoubtedly want to add other sizes and types.

Tool	Our choices	Bevel	Uses and comments
GOUGE	¾" and ½" and spindle ½" bowl	30–45°	You'll probably use these first and most often. Bigger gouges do roughing work; smaller ones handle details and fine cuts. Deep-flutes and short-beveled, bowl gouges remove stock quickly in faceplate work.
SKEW CHISEL	½" and 1"	20–25°	After you've rounded down stock with a gouge, you use a skew to smooth it out and shape it. A skew can make V-cuts, beads, and shoulders. The cutting edge is skewed 30–35° from the tool's end; the bevel measures twice as long as the tool is thick.
PARTING TOOL	¾" with a ⅛" diamond-point tip	25°	Parting tools do best at detail work. They also come in handy for "parting" tasks such as separating a small part from the main body of stock. The thickness of the tool's tip—⅛" or ¼"—determines the width of the cut.
SCRAPER	½" round-nose	15–20°	The round-nose scraper, a good general-purpose tool for faceplate work, also makes coves and grooves on spindles. If you decide to buy a second scraper, get a 1" flat-nose. Other popular scrapers have hooklike blades specially shaped for turning inside bowls.

HOW TO SHARPEN TURNING AND CARVING TOOLS

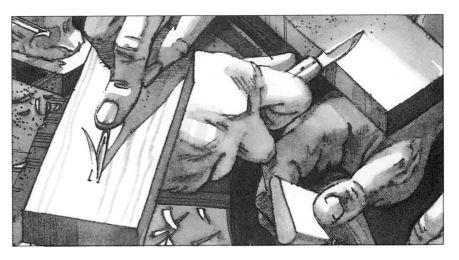

Carving or turning wood with dull tools is like trying to cut tough steak with a butter knife. You simply don't get the desired results. To help you start sharp and stay sharp, we paid a visit to two accomplished craftsmen— one a turner, the other a carver—who know full well the value of sharp tools. Starting with turning tools, here's what they had to say about getting a good edge.

Tips for getting an edge on your turning tools

From this secluded shop in the northern woodlands of Wisconsin, Rus Hurt quietly turns objects of exquisite beauty. Many of these pieces will find their way into art galleries and juried shows. Not bad for someone who describes himself as "just another guy out in the tules who happens to turn well."

workshop. His first lesson: How to properly sharpen your turning tools. Says Rus: "With dull tools you don't cut the wood; you tear it off, and that's how not to have fun with turning."

Determine the correct bevel and profile for your tools

After buying a turning tool, Rus regrinds its tip to match its intended purpose. "New tools are ground by machines that don't produce the necessary angles for smooth cutting," Rus said. "With most tools, the tips are too blunt, so you have to lengthen the bevel and taper the profile slightly."

For example, the photos *below* show the degree to which Rus grinds away the ears of his gouges and increases the length of the bevels to match the work at hand.

continued

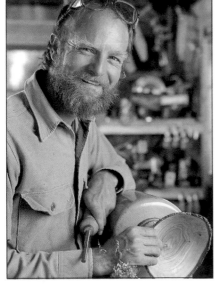

Rus Hurt

Rus especially enjoys passing along the secrets of his craft to aspiring turners at seminars and in one-on-one sessions in his own

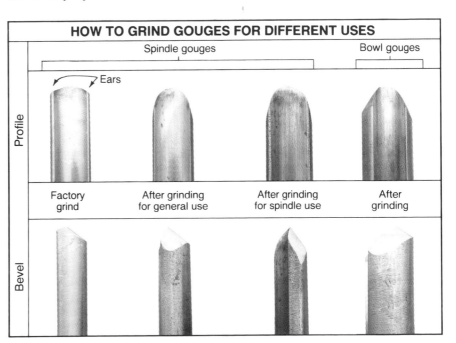

HOW TO GRIND GOUGES FOR DIFFERENT USES

	Spindle gouges			Bowl gouges
Profile	Factory grind (Ears)	After grinding for general use	After grinding for spindle use	After grinding
Bevel				

HOW TO SHARPEN TURNING AND CARVING TOOLS
continued

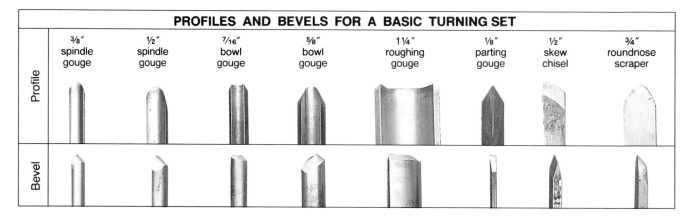

	PROFILES AND BEVELS FOR A BASIC TURNING SET							
	³⁄₈″ spindle gouge	½″ spindle gouge	⁷⁄₁₆″ bowl gouge	⅝″ bowl gouge	1¼″ roughing gouge	⅛″ parting gouge	½″ skew chisel	¾″ roundnose scraper
Profile								
Bevel								

Before grinding, mark the tool's new profile with a pencil.

Keep the tool moving as you grind it to avoid overheating.

As you can see, he recommends using a long bevel when you're turning spindles, and a shorter one for bowl turning. If you use a single gouge for both purposes, a compromise such as the "general use" example will work well.

To show you how to grind a variety of turning tools, we asked this longtime turner to select eight basic tools (see photos *above*). "With these tools, most turners can tackle 90 percent of all projects," he said.

Note: *Rus's bevel grinds should work well for you if you adjust the height of your lathe so the headstock center is about 1″ above your elbow.*

Rough-grind your tool tips into shape

Using the photos *above* as your guide, mark the necessary profile as shown *top left*. Then, hold the tip of the tool as shown *left*, and grip its handle with your other hand.

After grinding the ears (outer corners of the edge) down to the line, grind the entire bevel in one smooth and continuous motion by swinging the handle in an arc and simultaneously rolling the tool's edge. The new profile should be a smooth arc, with equal amounts of steel removed from both sides. Try to minimize the number of facets (flat spots) on the bevel.

Put the final edge on the tool

With the tip now reshaped, you shouldn't have to rough-grind the tool again unless you nick or damage it in some way. You need only refine the bevel with the fine

How to keep your tools cool when rough-grinding

Whenever you grind a tool, try not to overheat it. (When the steel turns blue, it has lost its temper and will not hold an edge.) Follow these pointers:
- Use a coarse stone.
- Keep the tool moving when it's against the stone.
- Be aggressive. Apply plenty of pressure to remove as much material as possible, then quickly get the tool off the stone before it overheats.
- Dip the tool in water frequently to lower its temperature.
- Because there's little steel near the cutting edge to dissipate heat, use a lighter touch when grinding near the tip.
- Practice your grinding on a piece of scrap steel. "I put in many hours at the grinding wheel before I became good," Rus reminded us, "and I still burn the steel occasionally."

stone of your grinding wheel. Start by touching the heel of the bevel to

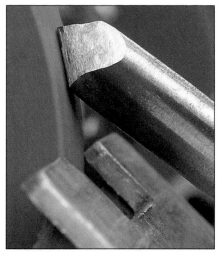

Touch the heel of the bevel to the grinder first, then ease the toe into the wheel before grinding the entire bevel. This helps you avoid burning the edge.

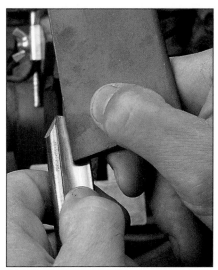

With a slipstone you can quickly remove the burr from the edge of a gouge.

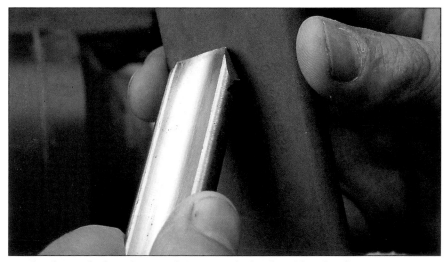

Stroke the tool's bevel several times with the flat side of a slipstone.

save you from damaging a turning with a dull tool. Just be careful not to cut yourself in the process!"

A proven system for sharpening carving tools

Harold Enlow, noted author and caricature carver, makes no bones about the importance of using sharp carving tools. "Some people complain that I put too much sharpening information in my books [he's published eight titles so far], but I ignore 'em because their tools are usually real dull," he told us with a chuckle.

Harold Enlow

To see firsthand Harold's tried-and-true sharpening technique, we paid a visit to his shop in the Ozark Mountains of northern Arkansas. Here's what we learned.

If you carve softer woods, grind the bevel longer

"I would guess that 90 percent of the wood being carved is soft—mostly basswood," said Harold. "But most carving tools come with a short bevel that works OK with harder woods, but not with softer woods. After I grind the bevel longer, the tool slices through these soft woods much more easily, with no damage to the cutting edge."

Note: *The following procedures work well with chisels, gouges, and bench knives. V-tools require special treatment (see page 15).*

As shown in the drawing on *page 14,* Harold lengthens the bevel on chisels and gouges so it's equal to the width of the tool. To do this, *continued*

the stone as shown *top left* and ease the rest of the bevel into the grinding wheel. Smooth the entire bevel in a continuous arcing motion, and use a light touch. Again, aim for one continuous facet.

"I'm usually done at this point unless I'm turning a fragile burl or expensive piece of stock,"said Rus. "In these instances, I'll hone the edge for an extra margin of sharpness." To do this, Rus gives the inside of the edge a few strokes with a coarse India slipstone as shown *top right* to remove the fine burr left from grinding. Then, he also strokes the bevel a few times

as shown *above*, rolling the tool as he pulls it.

Two more tips from Rus

"Buy high-speed steel (HSS) tools. You'll more than make up the higher cost in time saved from not having to resharpen them as much. And, HSS tools resist burning better than carbon-steel tools."

"Get in the habit of touching the tip of your turning tool with your finger each time you're ready to turn with it. The edge of a sharp tool will drag when you lightly run your thumb perpendicularly over the edge. You'll get a good feel for what 'sharp' means, and it could

HOW TO SHARPEN TURNING AND CARVING TOOLS
continued

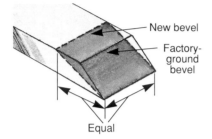

New bevel —
Factory-ground bevel —
Equal

use a coarse grinding wheel to remove steel from the bevel's heel. As you grind closer to the toe, be careful not to scorch the thin edge. (See the tips on *page 12* for more advice on keeping your tools cool.)

Harold guides the tool by grasping its handle in one hand, and putting downward pressure on the tool with the thumb of his other hand as shown *below*. This way, your thumb tells you when the tool gets too hot. When you're done grinding, there should be a slight burr on the edge (opposite the bevel surface). "At every stage of sharpening, I always feel for that fine burr. Then, and only then, can you be sure that you've reached the edge," Harold told us.

Use sharpening stones to flatten and smooth the bevel.

Harold goes directly from the coarse grinding wheel to a coarse

Your thumb helps steady the tool as you grind it, and also warns you when the tool gets too hot.

India bench stone to flatten the bevel and remove scratches. First, he applies an oil (motor oil or automatic-transmission fluid) to the stone and lays the bevel flat on the stone as shown *below*. "It's important that you apply plenty of pressure as you stroke the bevel several times," Harold said. "Your knuckles should turn white."

When working on a stone, remember to push and pull the tool for speedy metal removal. With gouges, you need to roll the tool as you push and pull it.

Hold the bevel flat on the stone as you stroke it heelfirst.

A note about the stones: "I use an India stone with a coarse and fine side, and a hard Arkansas stone, but most any combination of coarse, fine, and hard stones will work," Harold told us. "Other carvers get good results with diamond stones, water stones, you name it."

As you work, frequently check the tool's bevel in a strong sidelight. When most of the scratches disappear, switch to a fine stone. Harold repeats this process on the fine side of his India stone. When he's satisfied that he's removed all of the visible scratches, he removes the burr by stroking it lightly once or twice along the fine side of the stone. For gouges, use the long edge of the stone.

Next, Harold repeats everything he did on the fine side of the India stone on a hard Arkansas stone. "Some people skip this step and go directly to a strop [a leather strap with polishing compound on it] for

the final honing, but this step saves you time on the strop. And, the less time you spend on the strop the better, because stropping tends to round the edge slightly."

The final step—stropping

To polish the edge and remove any traces of a burr, Harold strokes both sides of the cutting edge on a strop charged with Zam polishing compound (see the Buying Guide *opposite* for a source). "You need to press hard and stroke each side of the tool five or six times," according to this seasoned carver. Because of its soft surface, you'll cut the strop if you try to push the tool across the leather, so only pull it along the surface.

As you strop the tool, mash the bits of compound into the leather surface. Press hard as you pull the tool along the strop five or six times.

Roll the concave side of a gouge as you pull it along the strop's edge. For each stroke, roll the tool completely from one corner of the edge to the other.

As shown in the photo *opposite, below,* Harold cuts off chunks of the compound and works it into his strop with the tool. When the Zam turns black, you'll need to add more compound. Polish the concave edge of a gouge by rolling it along the edge of the strop as shown *opposite bottom.*

How to tell when to resharpen your carving tools

To check his tools for sharpness, Harold shaves a few hairs off his arm. If the hairs don't shave easily, he gives the tool a few more strokes on the strop. Just be careful not to cut yourself.

Harold finds that he can restrop a tool two or three times before taking it back to the fine-India-stone stage of his sharpening process. "You don't have to go back to the grinder or coarse India stone unless the tool gets accidentally nicked."

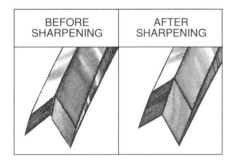

BEFORE SHARPENING	AFTER SHARPENING

How to get your V-tools shipshape

"In my seminars I find that few people know how to sharpen a V-tool," Harold said. "You can get by with a chisel or knife that's half-dull, but a V-tool has to be perfect or it'll give you fits."

To achieve victory with your V-tool, follow the sharpening sequence for other carving tools, but with these differences:

1. First, you need to check the V-tool's edge for squareness. If it looks like the example shown on the left side of the illustration *above,* you'll need to grind it square as shown on the right side of the same drawing. As also shown in this drawing, you should lengthen the bevels so they equal the width of one side of the V.

2. Check to make sure that the two edges of the tool meet in a

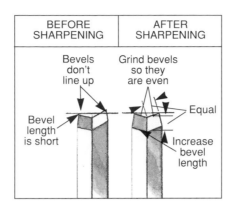

BEFORE SHARPENING	AFTER SHARPENING
Bevels don't line up	Grind bevels so they are even — Equal
Bevel length is short	Increase bevel length

Channel not centered

perfect V as shown in the "After sharpening" example *above.* (You may need a magnifying glass and strong light.) If they don't, you'll need to grind them into shape.

Doing this may prove impossible if the channel machined down the shank of the tool isn't centered as shown at *left.* So, check your V-tools for this defect before purchasing them.

3. On small V-tools, you may want to skip the grinding-wheel stage and only work on India stones to help you maintain control over steel removal.

4. Use thin, hard Arkansas slipstones to remove the burr on V-tools as shown *below.* For small

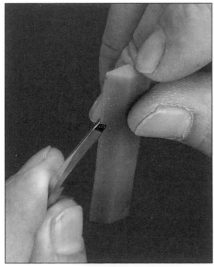

A slipstone with a fine point helps you deburr the inside edge of a V-tool.

Gently round the outside of the V on a fine India stone, so it matches the roundness on the inside of the V.

V-tools, Harold sharpens and shapes his slipstone on an India stone to make the slipstone's edge fit into the V.

5. The inside of the V should have some roundness, so slightly round over the outside of the V on a fine India stone to match the inside as shown *above.*

To polish the inside surface of a V-tool, pull it along the strop's edge.

6. To polish the inside surfaces of the V-tool, stroke it along the edge of a strop as shown *above.*

Buying Guide
• **Zam polishing compound.** For current price, contact Laughlin Woodcarving Supply, Route 6, Box 147, Harrison, AR 72601, call 501-741-4757.
• **Two-sided India stone.** One 8x2x1" coarse/fine stone, item No. 08M04.01. To order, contact Garrett Wade, 161 Avenue of the Americas, New York, NY 10013, or call 800-221-2942. (All types of sharpening accessories available. Call 212-807-1155 for information.)

TURNING TIPS AND TECHNIQUES

From stave-bowl construction and a simple method for great bowl design to drying green-turned bowls in a microwave oven and more, this section is chock-full of handy hints and great techniques for beautiful turning results.

GREEN-WOOD TURNING

Woodworkers usually avoid working with green wood. When it comes to turning, though, lots of people actually prefer it. You may join that crowd after you find out how easy and satisfying green-wood turning can be. We've gathered some pointers to help you get started. Once you begin, the absolute pleasure of it will keep you going.

If you think of woodturning as a grit-your-teeth showdown against a hard, unyielding chunk of wood, it's time to turn green. Green wood, that is.

When *WOOD*® magazine Senior Editor Pete Stephano had to have a large catalpa tree in his yard cut down a while back, we had a chance to practice with a couple of the logs. We marveled at the almost magical power our lathe and turning tools seemed to have in the freshly cut wood. Give it a try yourself. You'll find such sheer pleasure in turning green wood that you may figure that's the only reason to do it.

You'll soon discover it's not. For instance, you'll find green wood readily available, maybe as close as your backyard. When you buy it, green wood often sells for less than seasoned or kiln-dried wood. Sometimes it's free.

You can't beat it for workability, either. Tools practically glide through green wood. And, they hold their edges longer, too. You'll spend more time turning and less time sharpening after you join the Green Revolution.

Actually, green-wood turning shouldn't be called a revolution; it goes back to the very roots of turning. Before motor-driven lathes and high-quality steel tools, woodworkers turned green wood out of necessity. They simply did not have the power or the tools to turn hard, dried wood.

Gather some green wood

Tree surgeons and landscaping firms, firewood dealers, contractors clearing land, broken branches in your backyard—all are potential sources of green logs or limbs. Many specialty wood dealers sell greenwood blanks for turning, also.

But, won't it warp?

You probably have one main concern about turning green wood. You're afraid that you'll invest time and effort in turning a terrific bowl that will just end up warping, aren't you? In fact, that's exactly what's going to happen.

The secret to success lies in expecting warpage and having a plan for dealing with it. You have two choices. First, you can rough-turn a thick-walled bowl, let it season (and warp), and then finish-turn it months later to end up with a round bowl. Or, you can turn a finished form with thinner walls. As it seasons, warpage will become another element of the bowl's design.

Seven tips to start with

No matter which approach you want to try, here are some tips to get you started.

1. Use a small faceplate, one about 3" in diameter. Attach it to the bowl-bottom side of the blank so that you can turn the inside and outside in one mounting.

2. Screw the lathe faceplate to the bandsawed blank. Although many turners mount dried blanks with adhesives, *don't count on glue or tape for mounting green wood*. Joint failure could injure you or others in your shop.

3. Make sure you align two of the screws along the grain. Those two will serve as index marks for a bowl you'll remount to finish.

4. Stand outside the firing zone when you start the lathe. That's always a good safety rule, but with green wood, it may keep you drier, too. Your spinning blank can sling off a surprising quantity of moisture (and maybe a few insects). The amount of slung sap depends on the kind of wood you're turning and its freshness.

continued

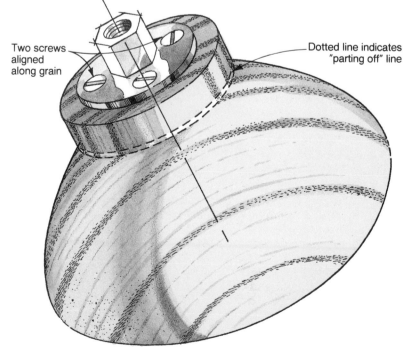

Two screws aligned along grain

Dotted line indicates "parting off" line

GREEN-WOOD TURNING
continued

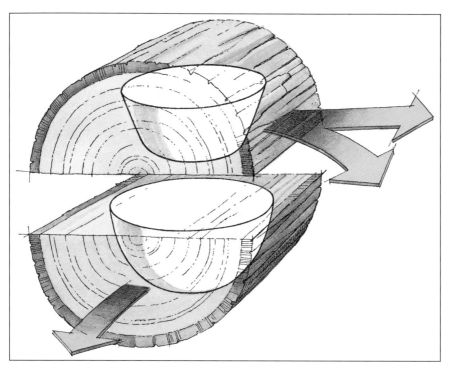

5. Keep your tools sharp. Don't think that because green wood cuts easily you can get by with dull tools. They'll bend the resilient fibers rather than cutting them. Your bowl-turning gouge will suffice for the green bowl.

6. Turn the inside and outside in one session. If you're roughing out a bowl to be finish-turned after seasoning, establish the general shape at this stage. Leave the wall thickness about 1/10 of the bowl's diameter. If you're turning a finished bowl, turn to your usual wall thickness, but leave a little extra material on the base or foot.

7. Strive for uniform wall thickness to promote even moisture loss during seasoning. This minimizes cracking.

Some tips for seasoning your bowl

1. If you rough-turned your bowl to finish later, here are some seasoning tips. Skip down to the bottom tip if you turned a finished form.

2. Unscrew the turning from the faceplate. Apply a sealer such as paste wax to moderate moisture loss and prevent checking and cracking. Store the bowl away from air movements and extreme temperature variations until it's ready to re-turn.

3. Check the bowl daily for the first week or so. Cracking or checking indicates that the wood is drying too quickly; apply more wax or sealer. If you live in a dry

climate, put the bowl inside a plastic bag, too. Your bowl will be ready for finish-turning in about three months.

4. Monitor the seasoning more accurately with a scale indicating grams or fractions of an ounce, if you want to be precise. Record the date and bowl weight when seasoning starts. Then, weigh it periodically and note the readings. When the weight remains stable for several days, complete the bowl.

5. Rejoin the bowl and faceplate after seasoning. Drive screws into the existing holes along the grain and redrill the others. Now, with your gouge and scrapers, bring the turning into round again. Complete the shape, sand, and finish as you would any bowl.

6. If you turned a finished bowl in the first session, sand it with progressively finer sandpaper while still on the lathe. Since you won't be re-turning it, this will be your last chance to put a fine surface on

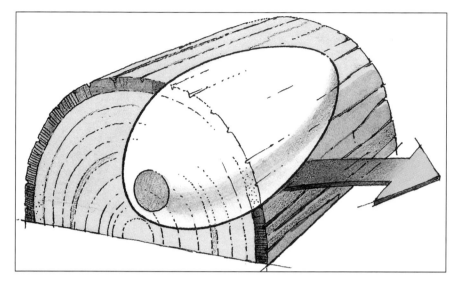

it. Many woods polish up nicely when green. Remove the bowl from the faceplate and set it aside in a draft-free spot to season.

Watch for checking and cracking as above, though the thinner more flexible wall section of the finished form won't be so likely to crack. After it seasons about three months, sand the bottom flat, and then finish your one-of-a-kind bowl as you prefer.

Lots of choices for displaying grain

While green wood is a natural for turning bark-edged bowls, that's not your only choice. Depending on the wood, just flipping the blank over could result in a much more dramatic turning; it's all in knowing how the turning's position in your chunk of wood affects grain display.

In any position, color variations between heartwood and sapwood provide one design aspect. Consider cracks, isolated discolorations, or figure in the wood, also. Do you want to minimize their impact or highlight them as effective design elements?

The accompanying illustrations, adapted from Arizona turner Todd Hoyer's study "Wood and Its Relationship to the Turned Object," show turned vessels placed in the log different ways. The corresponding photos show the resulting grain pattern for each turning.

Heartwood for the rim

An open bowl with the rim at the heartwood side of a halved log brings out the familiar saddle-shaped grain pattern in Photo 1. This placement yields the largest possible bowl from a given log.

Changing the bowl shape changes the grain display with this positioning. Instead of flaring the bowl rim outward, turn it inward; you'll see two bull's-eyes opposite each other with saddles between them.

Heartwood for the base

To bring out the parallel-ring pattern shown in Photo 3, orient your bowl with the base at the heartwood side of your blank.

You'll turn natural-edge bowls as in Photo 2 or those with bark edges with this placement, too.

Log size influences the shape of the rings that you'll end up with. They'll fall into an oval pattern when you turn a small-diameter log. But, you'll develop a round pattern (or more nearly so, anyway) in a bowl from a larger one.

Try varying the relationship between log diameter and bowl size for different effects. Bowl shape, however, doesn't alter grain display when you locate the base in the heartwood.

Yearn to turn an urn?

An urn or vase will display continuous parallel rings around the outside whether the top is at the heart side or bark side. Shape won't alter it, either.

Want a light sapwood highlight on one side at the widest diameter, as shown in Photo 4? Just locate your vase or bowl along the log's axis (end grain at top and bottom), but offset it toward the outside of the log.

ZAP! DRY GREEN BOWLS IN MINUTES

Drying your green-turned bowls by microwave isn't foolproof by any means—it takes a little testing. But when it works, great hoppin' microwaves, do you ever get quick results!

Walt Panek's house has a well-worn path between shop and kitchen. It's not that this Kingsport, Tennessee, woodworker works up an unusually large appetite from his hobby. On the contrary, it's because the kitchen microwave serves double-duty now that Walt

has discovered that it can actually dry his green turnings.

"A few years back, I used the microwave only to 'treat' the occasional rough-turned bowl or vase that I made from chunks of an insect-infested log. Then, I would set the pieces aside to season until they were dry enough to finish-turn," Walt recalls. "When I microwaved them, though, I noticed that the pieces came out of the oven considerably lighter, and with no ill effects. The microwave was drying the wood. So, I began to experiment a little more."

After successfully drying rough-turned bowls, Walt took the next logical step in his experiment. "I completely finish-turned a bowl to its final thickness before microwave-drying. I learned that I didn't have to leave the walls a uniform thickness to prevent warpage, as with the traditional finish-turn, then air-dry method," he notes. "I found that I could turn the walls to any desired thickness or a combination of thicknesses within the same turning. For example, if I wanted to leave a thick, heavy base on a bowl for stability, I could do it without fear of the base cracking."

Discovery after discovery marked Walt's continuing experiments. "I found out that besides being faster, microwave-drying has other interesting advantages," he continues. "For instance, sometimes when finish-sanding a green-wood turning on the lathe, developing heat caused checks and surface cracks to show up. But, I found that even fairly large cracks usually disappear in the microwaving cycle. And, frequently small checks will appear during the microwaving, but these also disappear within a few hours. This is probably due to the dry wood regaining moisture from the air, which swells the fibers and closes the cracks."

Bendable bowls

An air-dried, green-turned bowl always distorts a little. And, according to Walt, distortion occurs in microwaving, too. "The microwave-dried bowl won't go out of shape as much, though. Also, you can return it to the original shape by applying hand pressure immediately after you take the still-hot bowl from the oven. And, if you want, you can create some interesting shapes with the hot, plastic-like wood," he adds. "I've made wavy edges, a pour spout, and even pushed a bowl into an extreme oval. Naturally, the thinner the bowl, the easier it bends and holds its shape. All wood responds differently to shaping, however. I've noticed that apple works well."

Walt observed another interesting phenomenon when he turned a natural-edge bowl—one with the bark left intact. He discovered that microwaving makes the bark stay on better. "After microwave drying, the bark won't be as fragile, either. And, the sapwood, which I've found to be soft and pulpy before drying in the microwave, becomes firm afterward."

Pick your approach to microwaving

In microwave-drying green-wood turnings, you can choose one of two methods—the cautious approach or the go-for-it-all route.

Walt Panek dries green-turned bowls in the kitchen.

The first almost guarantees you a round bowl. That's because it basically follows the traditional method: rough-turning a green blank to from ¾" to 1" wall thickness, microwave-drying, then finish-turning and sanding. The difference is time—instead of several months of drying, it takes less than an hour!

In the go-for-it-all method, you aim to turn the green-wood bowl to finish thickness (usually from ⅛" to ⅜"), microwave dry, then sand. You end up with a finished bowl in a fraction of the time you're accustomed to.

When Walt practices the go-for-it-all method, he adds an unusual twist. "If I want to sand the bowl while it's still on the lathe, I apply a coat of sealer, sand it, then dry it in the microwave. The sealer seems to make the sanding easier, and it doesn't alter the drying time or the results," he notes.

In his experiments with his 650-watt oven, Walt found that the actual drying time, as well as oven setting needed, varies with the type of wood, its moisture content, and the bowl's wall thickness. "For one of my typical bowls—turned from fresh-cut maple to a ¼" wall thickness—I start with a four-minute drying cycle at a 40 percent power setting," he says. "There may be some signs of moisture escaping from the end grain—water vapor and hissing, popping sounds. I closely watch the bowl on the initial cycle to be sure there is no excessive steam escaping or moisture boiling out. If there is, the setting is too high," Walt advises. (See the chart on *page 22* for comparable settings on other microwaves.)

"After the first heat cycle, I remove the bowl from the oven and check the temperature by feel. If it's too hot to hold comfortably in my hand, I reduce the percentage setting on the next cycle," he continues. "Otherwise, after about a five-minute cooling cycle, I reheat for another four minutes."

After the second or third heat/cool cycle, the Tennessee turner quite often spots small checks appearing on the bowl's surface near the end grain. His experience tells him that they're nothing to worry about. They simply disappear. "I've even closed large or excessive cracks by putting the bowl under cool running water for a few seconds," Walt says.

The whole microwave-drying process takes three to four heat/cool cycles to dry most bowls, according to Walt. How can you tell when they're dry? "When you don't see any more signs of moisture escaping from the end grain and the bowl feels warm and dry to the touch," he advises.

"If I decide to reshape the bowl after it's dry, I have to get it hot again," Walt continues. "What has worked for me is to put it back in the microwave for one minute on high (100 percent). That makes most pieces flexible enough to hand-bend or clamp into shape. To make sure a bowl stays round, turn it upside down on a flat surface and clamp it overnight."

Walt finishes his bowls after they have cooled by power-sanding them with adhesive-backed disks to remove any raised grain or water stains. And, there's a bonus at this stage, too. "Sanding goes easy. Due to the wood's extreme dryness, the paper doesn't load up," he says. "After sanding, I normally apply an oil finish, but I've used varnish, lacquer, and wax, too."

continued

ZAP! DRY GREEN BOWLS IN MINUTES
continued

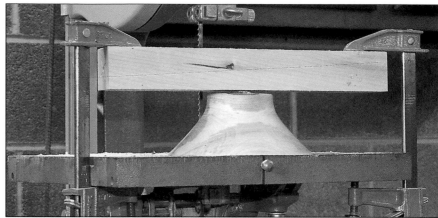

Clamping a bowl overnight after microwaving helps keep it round.

Avoiding disaster

Walt's wife, Sally, has a long memory. He says she can't forget his most dramatic disaster in microwave drying—and neither will he. "I had a 12" diameter by 5" deep spalted maple bowl that I turned to a uniform ⅛" wall thickness. I put it in the microwave as usual, but I inadvertently set the oven on 100 percent [high] rather than on 40 percent, and left the room. I returned in less than five minutes and the kitchen smelled like it was on fire. It wasn't, but my bowl had charred to the point that there was a hole all the way through one side," Walt chuckles. "The smell of burnt wood lingered in the oven for about three weeks, even with the door left open. That served as a real reminder to keep my mind on what I was doing when working with the microwave."

In addition to the chance of burning caused by missetting the controls, microwave-drying does present a few other, if small, problems. According to Walt, if the bowl is heated at too high a percentage setting on the initial cycle, it's more likely to have large cracks appear. Too, some wood may honeycomb, that is, develop a multitude of small fractures in a fanlike formation from the center to the outer edges. After regaining moisture from the atmosphere, the cracks may close. Or, especially on thicker-walled bowls, they may not.

"And, some light-colored woods will discolor where the moisture escapes from the end grain," says Walt. "This can sometimes be sanded off, but not always."

Walt has a final word of advice, too. "Get to know your microwave and its settings. But don't be afraid to experiment. I'm glad I did because this drying technique has greatly increased my enjoyment and capabilities in woodturning.

How to translate microwave settings

Nancy Byal, executive food editor for *Better Homes & Gardens®* magazine, says that most microwave ovens fall into the following power categories: 600- to 700- watt ovens (High), 400- to 550- watt ovens (Medium), and 400- watt ovens (Low). "In general, high-watt ovens require shorter cooking times," she says.

To determine your oven's output wattage, check the owner's manual or the oven label on the back of the appliance. If you can't find the rated wattage, you can figure it out (this test won't work at high altitudes).

In a 2-cup measure, heat 1 cup tap water (about 70°), uncovered, on 100% power (high). If the water boils in under three minutes, your oven probably has 600 watts or more. If the water takes longer than 3 minutes to boil, your oven produces less than 600 watts.

According to Nancy, microwave settings, unlike a conventional gas or electric oven, have little direct relationship to heat. Power levels, expressed as 100% or high, 70% or medium-high, etc., refer to the amount of time the oven is generating microwaves. For example, 50% means half the time the oven is on it is generating microwaves.

Here's help in translating the settings on your microwave or comparing them to those mentioned.

Comparative microwave settings*			
Percent	**Number**	**Word rank**	**Term**
100	10	High	Cook
70	7	Medium-high	Roast
50	5	Medium	Simmer
30	3	Medium-low	Defrost
10	1	Low	Warm

*Medium-power and low-power microwaves require a longer time to cook than high-power units on any of the above settings. Also, if your microwave has settings that differ from those above—such as "fish/poultry" or "desserts"—you may have to arrive at more quantitative settings by experimenting with the cup of boiling water test described above, or refer to the manufacturer's cookbook or owner's manual to find a comparable relationship.

Marlen Kemmet, *WOOD*® magazine's how-to editor, covers himself with shavings as he turns a bowl from fresh-cut elm. Following Walt Panek's step-by-step microwave-drying technique, the bowl turned out great.

Art director Lee Gatzke microwave-dries his green-turned bowls wrapped in three layers of newspaper—but only on defrost for short times. The paper wicks away and absorbs moisture, keeping the inside of the oven dry.

Now, I'm able to finish a project in one continuous operation. The only limits are my imagination and the size of my wife's microwave."

Microwaving tips from the *WOOD*® magazine shop

From our experiments and talks with microwave experts in the *Better Homes & Gardens*® Test Kitchen, we have found that the following factors can affect your microwave-drying of green-turned bowls:

Microwaves penetrate porous materials more easily than dense materials. Therefore, a dense wood such as Osage orange (.76 specific gravity) would take twice as long to dry as cottonwood (.37 specific gravity), if they were equally green to begin with.

The initial temperature of the wood affects the drying time. Try to start with wood that's at least room-temperature.

Hot spots prevent even drying. Since every microwave oven has its individual microwave pattern, you must observe for uneven distribution and place the bowl accordingly. To find out if your microwave has spots that are bombarded with more microwaves than other parts, watch food cook. Bubbles will first appear in a hot spot because it gets more microwaves. An accessory turntable will help distribute microwave action more evenly, except at the center of the item.

Following a short period of microwaving, let the bowl stand in the oven with the microwaves off. Because moisture attracts microwaves, parts of a bowl that may have a higher moisture content, such as a solid, elevated base, get hotter than wood with less moisture, such as thin walls. Letting it stand distributes the heat. On a bowl with base and walls of uniform thickness, it allows the greater heat accumulated on the edges to move to the center.

High altitude will influence your microwave. Slight changes in cooking times become noticeable at 2,500 feet above sea level and become dramatic above 5,000 feet. At 5,000 feet, water boils at 202° rather than the sea-level boiling point of 212°. In fact, the boiling temperature drops 2° for each 1,000-foot rise in altitude above sea level. Because of this lower temperature, increase the microwave time slightly. At altitudes above 7,500 feet, however, low air pressure causes faster moisture evaporation, so necessary microwave time actually shortens. At this altitude, you may want to wrap your green turned bowl in microwave-safe paper toweling to slow drying and stave off checking. It also may be necessary to reduce your microwave setting to compensate.

TURNING BETWEEN CENTERS

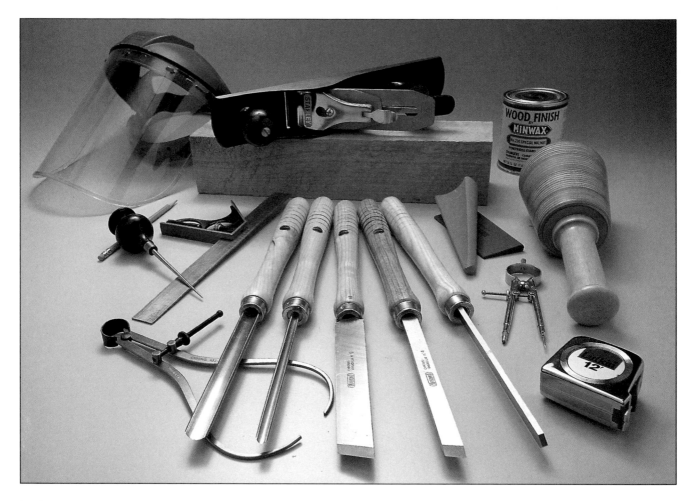

There's a lot to know about wood turning, a lot of territory to cover. After all, some people spend years mastering this truly artistic form of woodworking. We've decided to delve into turning between centers this time, and later on in the book we'll talk faceplate turning.

Here's what you'll need

The lathe plus five *turning chisels* will enable you to make all the cuts necessary to turn any between-centers project. A ½" gouge and a ¼" version of the same chisel serve double duty. They do the rough cutting necessary to round-down the turning square to a cylindrical shape. And they also come in handy when you want to

make a cove, or concave, cut. We use a *skew* that's anywhere from ½" to 1" wide to smooth the ridges left from rounding-down the stock with the gouge. And for making beads (the convex portion of turnings), we rely on a ½" diamond-point parting tool. This same tool also cuts grooves.

You'll also need the other tools and materials shown in the photo *above*. Note especially the *face shield,* which safeguards you against flying wood chips while you're operating the lathe. Wearing it is an absolute must. We'll talk about the uses of the other items later.

Laying out your turning project

As a woodturner, you need to develop the skill of making

templates. Why? Because the template serves as a valuable referencing aid. It allows you to check visually on the progress of your turning. Templates also allow you to reproduce several identical pieces of a given shape.

To fashion a template, start by cutting a ⅛" piece of plywood or hardboard to the length of the turning. (We use Baltic birch plywood for our templates because of its stability and light color.) Then, draw a line lengthwise down its center.

After doing this, if you don't have a scaled drawing to work from, draw the profile of the turning as best you can. Then continue to refine the shape until you have an attractive profile. If you do have a scaled drawing, transfer the outline

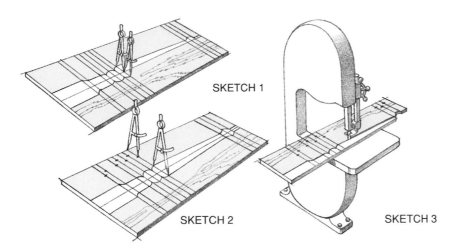

SKETCH 1

SKETCH 2

SKETCH 3

A

B

C

D

of the turning to graph paper and onto the template material.

Draw a line perpendicular to the center line at every point where the profile changes direction. Then, using a compass or dividers, transfer the points of intersection to the opposite side of the lengthwise line as shown in Sketch 1, *above.*

Once you're satisfied with the shape you've sketched, measure each diameter and transfer it to one edge of the template material as shown in Sketch 2. These marks allow you to set your outside calipers easily when checking the diameter of the turning at various points.

Now cut the template along the lengthwise line, make relief cuts, and saw along the profile line as shown in Sketch 3.

Preparing the stock for turning

How you go about this depends on whether you plan to do a fully turned project or one that's partially turned. In the photo sequence at right, we'll show you how to prepare both types. The first three photos apply to partially turned work and the second three apply to both.

1. With partially turned projects, it's important that the stock be square. If you're working with stock whose surfaces aren't at right angles to each other, follow this procedure, as shown in Photo A. Clamp the stock in a vise and plane one surface smooth. (You can also joint the surface smooth if you have a jointer.) To check the surface for true, hold the blade of a try or combination square directly on the surface and look for daylight along the blade.

2. Lay the stock on a plywood scrap so that one edge of the stock overlaps the edge of the plywood. (The opposite edge of the plywood must be straight.) Then trace the outline of the stock, cut the waste material away, and fit the stock into the jig you've just created. (Make sure the planed surface is on the bottom.) Now slowly and carefully pass the stock through a table saw as shown in Photo B. Note that we used a featherboard to help control the cut.

3. As soon as you have two sides of the stock squared up, you can then discard the jig and square up the other two surfaces with your table saw. Next, you need to square up the ends of the stock (Photo C). Doing this ensures that the turned portion will be at a right angle to the ends, and it will also help reduce vibration when you put the stock on the lathe and begin rounding down. Using your table saw miter gauge and a stop block, make both cuts.

4. Clamp the stock in a vise, and—using the blade of a square— draw diagonal lines from corner to corner on both ends of the stock, as shown in Photo D. An accurate centerpoint is important especially if you're doing a partially turned project. It ensures that the turned portion will be the same distance from each edge of the unturned

continued

TURNING BETWEEN CENTERS
continued

portion. It also lessens the amount of vibration during the rounding-down process.

5. Make a starter hole at the centerpoint of each end with an awl or center punch. Want to make the rounding-down process a little less bumpy and easier on your turning tools? If so, mark the turning's greatest diameter with a compass and mark a line just beyond the outside of the circumference line at each corner as shown in Photo E. (Experienced turners don't bother with this step, but it's worth knowing about.)

6. With the turning square held securely in a bench vise, remove the waste material with a bench plane as shown in Photo F. (Note that we're planing the stock at an angle rather than straight on.) Or, set your saw blade at a 45° angle, adjust the rip fence as needed, and run the stock through the table saw. If you're doing a partially turned project, you'll want to stop the cuts short of the shoulder.

Mounting the stock on the lathe

1. Begin by aligning the centerpoint of the stock with that of the drive center. Then, as in Photo G, tap the stock with a mallet until the drive center spurs engage the stock. Don't beat on the stock; that's not necessary, and it's hard on the headstock bearings. If you'd rather, you can also remove the drive center, saw shallow diagonal cuts from corner to corner with a handsaw, and tap the center into the stock.

2. Move the tailstock to just shy of the point at which the tailstock center and the stock meet, tighten the tailstock, and use your lathe's tailstock handwheel to move the center into the stock (Photo H). Here again, don't exert undue pressure; it's not necessary. If you don't have a ballbearing center (a good investment if you don't already own one of these nifty accessories), apply some paraffin wax to the stock where it meets the center to reduce friction and possible burning.

3. After tightening the tailstock and the center, move back up to the headstock. Wrap a piece of masking tape around the drive center, and mark one of the spurs and its corresponding location on the end of the turning, as in Photo I. This is insurance—just in case you have to remove the turning from the lathe before it's finished and have to remount it later. (If you wish, you can also permanently notch one spur with a file.)

4. We've included Photo J to show you the importance of having the tool rest parallel and close to the turning at all times. The rest should also be about halfway between the top of the turning and the centerpoint.

Note: *Make sure that you always shut off the lathe before moving the tool rest. Also rotate the stock to make sure it and the tool rest won't make contact.*

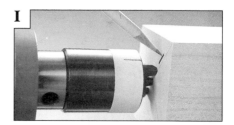

Rounding down and turning the stock

1. With the lathe set on a low speed (around 800 rpm), use a sharp gouge to begin the rounding-down process. Work slowly from the headstock end down, and don't try to remove too much material at once. Notice the angle at which the gouge is being held in Photo K. At this angle, you're cutting the stock rather than scraping it. See Photo R on *page 28* for an example of how the scraping action differs from the cutting action.

2. You'll have to move the tool rest several times while you're

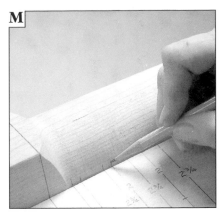

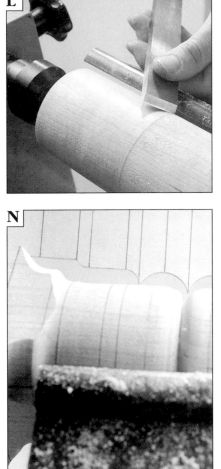

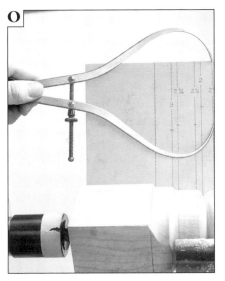

rounding down. Be sure to keep it close to the stock; this gives you greater control of the tool. If you want to put a mirrorlike sheen on the cylinder, hold the skew as shown in Photo L, with the bevel rubbing the cylinder and the heel of the blade doing the cutting. Done correctly, this procedure all but eliminates sanding.

3. Now lay your template up against the turning, and transfer the marks on the template to the turning. Make sure when you do so that the end of the template aligns with the end of the stock. In Photo M, we marked the end of the shoulder using a combination square, then started the lathe and marked the other lines.

4. Position the template as shown in Photo N, then begin shaping the project. By sighting across the turning onto the template occasionally, you can tell when you're approaching the correct shape. This technique also keeps you from making incorrect cuts—a common occurrence, especially if you're a beginning turner.

5. As you approach the finished diameter of the various segments of

the turning, check your progress often with an outside calipers, as shown in Photo O. Simply adjust the calipers to match the marks on the template, and keep turning until the calipers slips around the portion of the turning you're checking.

6. You can make any between-centers project once you learn to make beads and coves. Be advised, though, you'll have to practice a lot to become good at making either. To make a bead, first lay your parting tool flat on the tool rest and score both lines that define the width of the bead (Photo P).

7. Then, make a mark at the center of the bead. Position the parting tool at a slight angle to the tool rest and a bit on edge as shown in Photo Q, then roll the tool toward the score mark. The tool will be almost as shown in

Photo P at the end of the roll. Make another, deeper score line and then another roll action cut. Repeat this process until the bead is formed.

8. To make a cove, position the gouge as shown in Photo R. Don't go so deeply that the gouge's edges catch the stock.

9. To smooth the edges of the cove, hold the gouge at the angle shown in Photo S. Work from the side in toward the center of the cove.

Finishing your turning project

1. With most woodworking projects, preparing the surface for a finish is a drag. Not so with wood-turning projects. The lathe does the work for you—and in a big hurry. Just lay in a supply of 80-, 100-, and 150-grit sandpaper
continued

TURNING BETWEEN CENTERS
continued

and begin sanding. By having the sandpaper beneath the turning, as shown in Photo T, you can monitor your progress. Keep the paper moving.

2. Once you've removed all the imperfections from the surface, stop the lathe and lightly hand-sand the turning in the direction of the grain with 150-grit. Holding your thumbs as shown in Photo U allows the paper to conform to the object's shape. This light sanding removes those barely visible sanding marks left from across-the-grain sanding.

3. Most turners like to finish their projects right on the lathe because it's so quick and easy. To protect your clothes and surroundings from splatters, set up some kind of a simplified finishing booth such as the one shown in Photo V. We usually use scrap cardboard. When applying the finish, be sure you hold the rag with both hands so you don't accidentally tangle it up in the lathe.

Should you scrape or cut?

Much has been written about whether or not novice wood-turners can learn to use their chisels properly as cutters rather than scrapers. Professional and experienced amateur woodturners use their tools to cut because that action leaves the surface of a turned project much smoother than the scraping action. The result: less time spent sanding the project and less distortion of the desired shape. We think even beginners should take the time to learn to turn the correct way—cutting. It takes longer to master this technique, but the quality of your work will show.

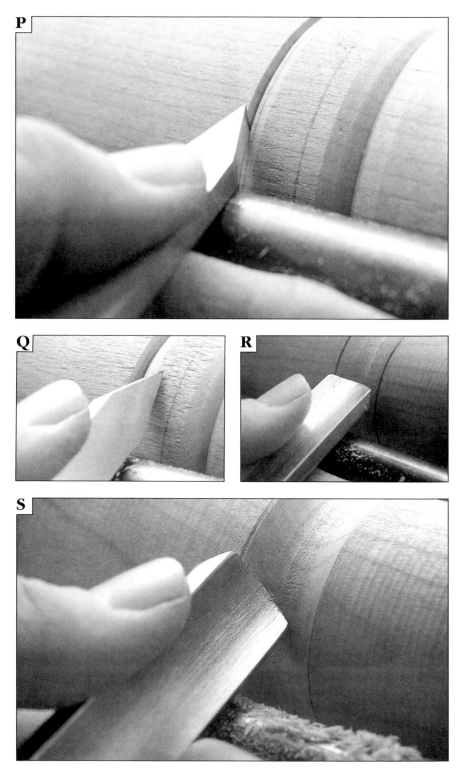

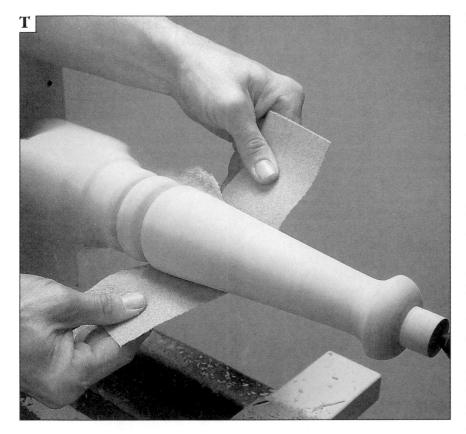

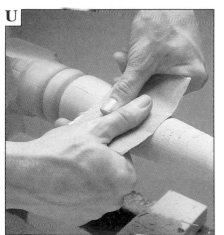

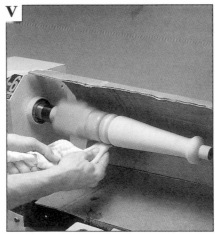

How slow should you go?

As a general rule, the larger the stock you're turning, the slower the lathe speed should be, especially during the rounding-down process. We've found that a speed of 800 to 1,000 rpm works well for rounding-down stock that's 2" or less. When we reach the cylinder stage, we increase the speed to around 1,500 rpm. It's not necessary to speed up the rpm for sanding.

Practice makes perfect

In wood turning, there's no better way to learn than by making the shavings fly. So, if you're just getting started, buy some scrap stock and practice your moves before you take on a for-real project.

The importance of sharp tools

Sharp lathe chisels make a world of difference to you as a turner. We hollow-grind ours on a coarse grinding stone at slow speed, then whet them with a slipstone. Sharp tools held at the correct angle will yield shavings, not sawdust.

What's available in turning stock

You can purchase turning squares (typically in ash, cherry, mahogany, maple, oak, and walnut at some lumber dealers and through mail order) or make your own from up to 3"-thick stock. Or, you can laminate several pieces of thinner stock.

To practice your technique, use 2–4" diameter tree limbs. The green wood turns easily, and costs you little or nothing.

BASIC STAVE-BOWL CONSTRUCTION

Along the eastern seaboard during the early years of American colonization, stave construction played an important role in commerce. In order to transport goods safely (and dryly) from the colonies to their trading partners across the ocean, merchants hired thousands of craftsmen to fashion wood containers and vessels of all kinds.

In colonial America, if you had the skills necessary to make watertight vessels, containers, or barrels to hold expensive dry goods, spices, or even spirits such as rum and whiskey, work was always available.

With the passage of time, though, along came the introduction of other packaging materials and labor-saving machinery to manufacture them. And with these improvements came the demise of

coopering, the trade devoted to shaping wooden staves into barrels, buckets, churns, and other such utilitarian items.

The tradition lives on, though, in some of the living history museums around the country and through the skills of some home woodworkers. Read on and we'll tell you what we have learned about stave construction—a truly fascinating woodworking technique—here in the *WOOD*® magazine shop.

And if you get as excited about what you learn as we did, you'll want to take a look at *pages 88-89.* There you'll find a great-looking bowl Design Editor Jim Downing dreamed up for you. Bet you can't resist building it!

The stave advantage

Let's face it! If you wanted, you could find several easier, less time-consuming ways to make a bowl. So why do serious craftsmen and

home hobbyist woodworkers go to such lengths to cut, join, and turn these multisided creations?

Several reasons, actually. First and foremost, stave construction allows you to create relatively large-diameter bowls using a minimum amount of material. Second, because you arrange and join the staves (short sections of

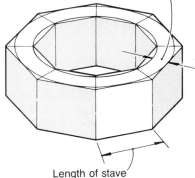

Maximum wall thickness

Length of stave

Anatomy of a stave bowl

Anyone who has ever sectioned an orange can appreciate the theory behind stave construction. Each *stave,* or section, when cut to the correct *bevel,* fits neatly next to adjacent pieces. And once you join them together, they form a multisided ring that, when turned, becomes the bowl's wall.

As you can see from the anatomy sketch *below,* a stave's grain direction can run either horizontally or vertically. The latter makes slightly stronger bowls because the staves come together edge grain to edge grain. And you can use either ¾" or 1¹⁄₁₆" stock for your bowl. The more sides the project has, the thinner the stock can be.

The bottom of the bowl, typically ⅜"- to ½"-thick solid stock, fits into a ⅛"- to ¼"-wide rabbet you cut into the wall. How deep you cut the rabbet depends on the bowl design. If you want to conceal the base, cut the rabbet the full thickness of the bowl bottom. To accent the base, cut it ⅛" or so shallower.

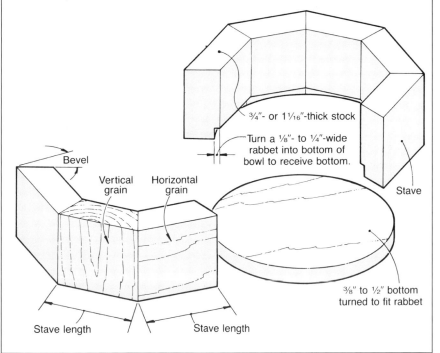

Bevel

Vertical grain

Horizontal grain

Stave length

Stave length

¾"- or 1¹⁄₁₆"-thick stock

Turn a ⅛"- to ¼"-wide rabbet into bottom of bowl to receive bottom.

Stave

⅜" to ½" bottom turned to fit rabbet

LENGTH OF STAVE			
Dia.	Number of Sides		
	8	10	12
4"	1²¹⁄₃₂"	1⁵⁄₁₆"	1¹⁄₁₆"
5"	2¹⁄₁₆"	1⅝"	1¹¹⁄₃₂"
6"	2½"	1¹⁵⁄₁₆"	1⅝"
7"	2²⁹⁄₃₂"	2¼"	1⅞"
8"	3⁵⁄₁₆"	2¹⁷⁄₃₂"	2⅛"
9"	3¾"	2¹⁵⁄₁₆"	2⁷⁄₁₆"
10"	4⁵⁄₃₂"	3¼"	2¹¹⁄₁₆"
11"	4⁹⁄₁₆"	3⁹⁄₁₆"	2¹⁵⁄₁₆"
12"	5"	3²⁹⁄₃₂"	3⁷⁄₃₂"

MAXIMUM WALL THICKNESS*			
Dia.	Number of Sides		
	8	10	12
4"	⅝"	1¹⁄₁₆"	⁴⁵⁄₆₄"
5"	¹⁹⁄₃₂"	2¹⁄₃₂"	1¹⁄₁₆"
6"	⁹⁄₁₆"	⅝"	⁴³⁄₆₄"
7"	¹⁷⁄₃₂"	¹⁹⁄₃₂"	2¹⁄₃₂"
8"	3¹⁄₆₄"	⁹⁄₁₆"	4¹⁄₆₄"
9"	2¹⁄₆₄"	¹⁷⁄₃₂"	⅝"
10"	⅜"	½"	³⁹⁄₆₄"
11"	2¹⁄₆₄"	3¹⁄₆₄"	¹⁹⁄₃₂"
12"	⁵⁄₁₆"	¹⁵⁄₃₂"	3⁷⁄₆₄"

* ¾" stock shown; add ⁵⁄₁₆" if you use 1¹⁄₁₆" stock.

wood) end grain to end grain or edge grain to edge grain, the finished project displays only beautiful face grain.

Stave bowls also turn smoothly on the lathe and tend not to suffer from grain tearout during turning. Add to these advantages the design flexibility you have with stave construction, and it's easy to see why this technique fascinates woodworkers who take the time to learn it.

Project planning tips

Start by giving some thought to what function you want the bowl to serve as well as to its diameter and height. Next, decide the number of segments (staves) you want your bowl to have. Then refer to the chart *below* as a guideline:

Diameter of Bowl	Min. No. of Staves
6" or less	8
7"	10
0–12"	12

Once you've determined the number of staves needed, simply refer to the chart *above right.* It tells you how long to cut each stave.

And to find out the maximum wall thickness you have to work with on your particular bowl, see the other chart *above.* Keep in mind that with ¾"-thick staves, you have less design flexibility than if you select 1¹⁄₁₆" material.

Now that you know the maximum wall thickness, draw a full-size section view of the wall and bottom as shown on the *following page,* and experiment until you settle on a profile that appeals to you. Then, make a cardboard template of the shape for use later while turning.

continued

BASIC STAVE-BOWL CONSTRUCTION
continued

Get ready . . . get set . . . cut the staves

With the "book work" out of the way, now you're ready to make some sawdust. What kind depends on the wood species you choose for your bowl. Oak, walnut, cherry, ash, sassafras, and mahogany, just to name a few, make beautiful staved bowls, but give your favorite wood a try as well.

No matter which wood you select, though, make sure that it has been kiln-dried or thoroughly air-dried. Otherwise, the bowl's joint lines almost certainly will pull apart and ruin your project. Also take care to choose flat and defect-free boards. And since you have to be precise when cutting staves, reject warped or cupped stock. As Project Builder Jim Boelling would say, "You want the eye of the steak."

Prepare the stock for cutting

Start by selecting a grain direction for your bowl walls. If you're new to stave construction, you may want to go with vertically grained walls because they're stronger and easier to turn than horizontally grained ones. In addition, with the former, you won't have to worry as much about matching the grain from section to section.

If the grain will run vertically, use the following formulas to determine the length and width of board needed for your staves:

Length = *Height of bowl×no. of sides + 30% for waste*

Width = *Length of one stave + ¼"*

If you elect to go with a horizontally grained bowl, figure the length and width this way:

Length = *No. of staves×length of each + 30% for waste*

Width = *Height of bowl + ¼"*

Now, draw the outline of the stave material onto a board as shown in the Cutting the Eye from the Steak drawing *above right.* To

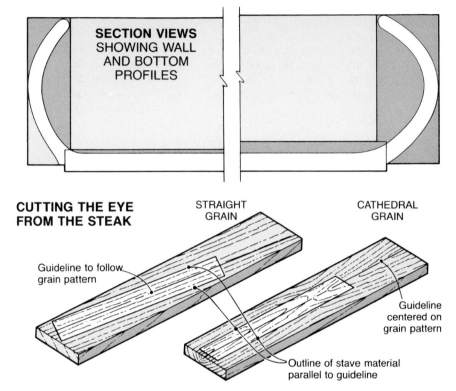

SECTION VIEWS SHOWING WALL AND BOTTOM PROFILES

CUTTING THE EYE FROM THE STEAK

STRAIGHT GRAIN

CATHEDRAL GRAIN

Guideline to follow grain pattern

Guideline centered on grain pattern

Outline of stave material parallel to guideline

ensure uniformity of grain pattern in the finished bowl, mark a guideline following the grain of the board. Then, complete the outline.

Cutting the staves to size

First, rip the stave material to rough width. (As you can see in the photo at *right,* we made our first cut with a circular saw guided by a straightedge. After one edge was straight, we made our second cut with a table saw, with the straightened edge toward the fence.) Now, cut the stock to length.

Next, refer to the chart at *right,* and select the proper angle of cut.

Carefully tilt the arbor of your saw to the appropriate angle as shown *opposite top.* If you have as much trouble as we do being precise in your settings, you'll appreciate knowing about an adjustable triangle, a drafting tool we ran across at our local art supply store. You can't beat it for quickly setting accurate angles

After laying out the location of the stave material, cut it to length and width. We straightened one edge with a circular saw.

STAVE ANGLES	
No. of Sides	**Cut Angle**
8	22.5°
10	18°
12	15°

With an adjustable triangle, set the blade angle carefully.

Dry-clamp the test staves to check for angle accuracy.

Even a small error in the blade angle can cause untold problems later when you glue up the staves. So always cut test staves and dry-clamp them as shown *below left*. If the toes of the staves touch each other, decrease the angle of your blade a bit and cut new test staves. And if the heels touch, you need to increase the blade angle slightly.

Note: Use a sharp saw blade when cutting staves. Otherwise, the joints won't fit together well.

Now, cut the staves to size. Here again, how you do this depends on the grain direction of the staves

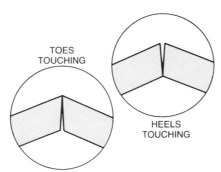

TOES TOUCHING

HEELS TOUCHING

when glued up. If it will run vertically, rip the stave material to its final width as shown *below left,* then reset the saw blade to cut at 90°, and crosscut the staves to length.

However, if the grain will run horizontally, follow this sequence: First, add an auxiliary fence to your saw's miter gauge. Then, raise the angled blade to cutting height, and pass the fence through the blade.

Now, mark a cutoff line on the auxiliary fence the correct distance from the inside edge of the saw blade (see sketch *bottom, left*). Make the first bevel cut at the end of the stock, then turn the board over, align it with the cutoff line, and make your second cut as shown *below.* Turn the board back over, trim off the end as shown in the bottom photo, and repeat this process for all the staves. Number each stave in the order it comes out of the stock.

Gluing up the staves

Even if you've worked carefully and made your cuts accurately, you

continued

For bowls with horizontal grain, make your first bevel-cut, mark a cutoff line on the auxiliary fence, flip the board over, and make the second cut.

For bowls whose sidewall grain will run vertically, bevel-rip the stave material to width. Then, crosscut each stave (at 90°) to length.

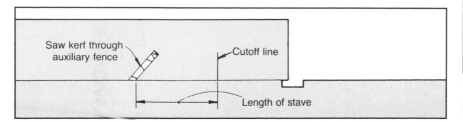

Saw kerf through auxiliary fence

Cutoff line

Length of stave

Now, flip the board over again and make another cut to reestablish the bevel angle. Repeat this process.

BASIC STAVE-BOWL CONSTRUCTION
continued

may have to make some minor adjustments prior to glue-up to make the staves fit perfectly. To check your staves for a good fit, dry-clamp them together. If you detect any openness in the joints, note whether you've got a toe-to-toe problem or a heel-to-heel problem.

Then, remove one or more of the staves, and sand both ends slightly to correct the problem. We've had good luck making these micro-adjustments with a table saw fitted with a disc sanding attachment as shown *below.*

After you're satisfied with the fit of the staves, apply glue to both ends of each as shown at *bottom.* Use band clamps to apply even pressure all around. Allow the glue to dry.

To make minor fitting adjustments, sand each end of one or two staves. Work carefully; it won't take much stock removal to make things right.

Note: Woodworker's glue works well in most situations, but we like 5-minute epoxy when we're in a hurry or when working exotic woods. Also, for maximum adhesion with exotics, wipe mating edges with alcohol before gluing.

Apply glue to both end surfaces of each stave. Then, band-clamp, making sure the tops remain flush.

Rough-turning the bowl

To prepare the staved ring for turning, begin by truing up the top of it. We do ours by chucking a disc sander into our drill press, locking the height, and rotating the blank as shown *below.*

Then, cut a ¾" plywood auxiliary faceplate ½" larger than the outside diameter of the staved ring. Center and screw a faceplate to the auxiliary faceplate, then turn the auxiliary faceplate to the outside diameter of the ring. Carefully center the bowl on the auxiliary faceplate, and glue and clamp the two together as shown in the photograph at *right.*

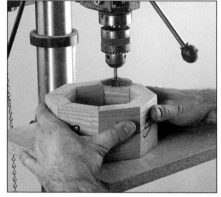

Sand the top of the bowl smooth. It's a breeze using the setup shown.

Now comes the creative part! Turn the bowl round with a spindle gouge, using the slowest speed on your lathe. (We like to remove material slowly to reduce the chances of tearout.) Then, with a parting tool, true up the bottom of the bowl as shown *right center.*

Now, reposition your tool rest, and cut a rabbet into the bottom of the bowl with a parting tool (see photo at *right*).

Note: At the joint lines between staves, you want the rabbet to be ⅛" to ¼" wide. How deep? That depends. If you don't want the bottom to show from the outside, cut the rabbet as deep as the bottom is thick. But if you'd rather

Center the bowl on the auxiliary faceplate, and clamp as shown.

After turning the bowl round with a spindle gouge, true up the bottom using a parting tool.

Again using a parting tool, cut a rabbet in the sidewall to accept the bottom of the bowl. See note at *left* for dimensions.

highlight the bottom as a design element, cut the rabbet a bit shallower.

Fitting the bottom to the bowl

After cutting the rabbet for the bottom, remove the faceplate from the auxiliary faceplate. Then, cut another auxiliary faceplate slightly larger than the inside diameter of the bowl. Attach it to the faceplate as you did before, and turn it round.

Cut a solid-wood bottom oversize (we usually use ¾"-thick material), and glue the centered auxiliary faceplate over the bowl bottom. Turn the bottom down to the thickness you want it (we like ⅜" to ½"-thick bottoms).

Now, turn the bottom until it fits snugly into the rabbet you cut into the bowl. Inspect the bottom often during turning to check it for size as shown *below*. Once you've got it right, glue the bottom into the rabbet, and let the glue dry.

For turning the sidewall, we had good results using a bowl scraper, and we smoothed the bottom with a skew.

Periodically check for a snug-fitting bottom while turning.

Caution: Wood does move! As you know, wood expands or contracts as dictated by existing conditions. We've talked to several woodworkers who specialize in stave bowls, and though they acknowledge this fact, they claim good results with solid-bottomed bowls. That's been our experience too. Keep these things in mind, though. The thicker the bottom and the larger the bowl diameter, the greater pressure there will be on the bowl wall. Also, when applying finish to your project, be sure to cover all surfaces evenly, including the bottom, to minimize uneven stress.

Final turning and finishing

Begin by parting off the auxiliary faceplate from the top of the bowl. Then, true up the top of the bowl, and turn the outside of the bowl to shape. Be sure to check the shape frequently with your template as shown *right*.

When you finish turning the outside of the bowl, reposition your tool rest, and shape the bowl's interior. We found that the bowl scraper shown *above* yielded good results on the wall and at the intersection of the bottom and the sidewall. For the bottom, we called on a skew.

From here on out, you finish stave bowls as you would any other turning project. We sand all surfaces with a succession of abrasive grits up to about 220, then chase away all the dust with a few blasts of air from our air compressor. After this, you can apply the finish of your choice on the lathe.

Work the outside of the bowl until it matches the shape of the template. Check the shape often with your template.

Now, separate the bowl from the auxiliary faceplate with a mallet and chisel. We made the split at the joint line of the ply closest to the bottom (Be careful you don't let the bowl drop and break.)

Then, sand the plywood from the bottom on a stationary belt sander, and remove the resulting scratches with an electric sander.

Inscribe your name and the date on the bottom of the bowl, apply a little finish, and you have a one-of-a-kind bowl that you or the lucky recipient will treasure forever. Happy turning!

A SUREFIRE TECHNIQUE FOR PLEASING BOWL DESIGN

Frustrated from figuring out what your bowl should look like? Here's help.

Dale Nish, the well-known woodturner, author, and educator from Provo, Utah, says "You could paint a good-looking, turned bowl black, and it would still be attractive." According to Dale, that's because a bowl's form should be appealing enough to stand by itself, yet display the wood to its maximum potential. But, coming up with great-looking bowl shapes that meet this standard perplexes even the best woodturners.

"I once attended a woodturning seminar taught by Bob Stockdale," Dale notes, "and someone asked him, 'Where do you get your ideas for shapes?' He said, 'I checked out a book on oriental porcelain from the library one time, and found out they had been copying me for 2,000 years!' "

That tongue-in-cheek reply actually was sound advice (see textbox, *opposite,* for design tips from the experts). Pleasing-to-the-eye pottery shapes show up in civilization after civilization throughout history. And, most all can be adapted from the potter's wheel to the lathe. But, unlike a potter, who has the luxury of shaping and reshaping as long as the clay remains wet, a woodturner can seldom change his mind. In bowlturning, advance planning becomes all-important.

Good bowl design begins with proportion

Some people possess a natural eye for shape and proportion. If you don't, there's plenty of hope. That's because—believe it or not—you can mathematically calculate pleasing-to-the-eye proportions.

The ancient Greeks perfected the "Golden Mean," a formula that

PROPORTIONING A BOWL WITH THE GOLDEN MEAN

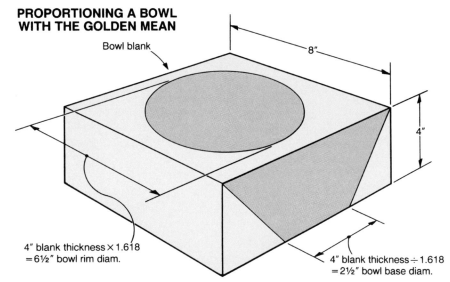

Bowl blank

8″

4″

4″ blank thickness × 1.618 = 6½″ bowl rim diam.

4″ blank thickness ÷ 1.618 = 2½″ bowl base diam.

utilizes the ratio 1:1.618 to find the length of the long side in relation to the short side of a rectangle. Furnituremakers have long relied on the formula.

But how does the Golden Mean help in bowlturning? With it, you can figure out such troublesome relationships as the diameter of the rim to the height of the bowl or the base diameter to the height.

Here's an example: Let's say you have a bowl blank 4" thick and 8"

square. You know the height cannot exceed 4", but to what diameter should you turn the bowl to maintain a pleasing proportion? Simply multiply 4×1.618 to find the diameter, which, in this case equals about 6½". For the diameter of the base, *divide* the 4" bowl height by 1.618. The result: about 2½" (see drawing, *above*).

These dimensions give you a beginning for a bowl with

Design tips from two top turners

Noted woodturners/authors Richard Raffan, from Australia, and Dale Nish, from Provo, Utah, teach novice turners. Here's their advice on bowl form:

What are the most common mistakes a beginning turner makes with form?

Raffan: Novice turners try to be too complicated when it pays to be as simple as possible. I made a great leap forward when I decided that I was getting too involved with reverse curves and such. When I started to do simple curves, I began to appreciate form. Beginners jump ahead too fast. They become so pleased with all the shapes gotten so quickly that they tend to make more use of the technique than the design.

Nish: Most beginning turners make the foot for the base of a bowl too large. The base, or the foot, diameter doesn't have to be any more than one-quarter to one third of the bowl's maximum diameter. If it's a functional piece, the base can go to half the maximum diameter. That gives it stability.

Should beginners avoid some types of forms?

Raffan: Go for open shapes. They're much, much easier to turn. It's far more difficult to create a tight curve that comes up and out from the base, then back in again, than an outflowing curve.

Study ceramics, especially Japanese pottery. The forms won't always be symmetrical, but you'll gain a sense of proportion. Remember, forms are pretty universal. You just learn to adapt.

Nish: Find a good shape and copy it! You'll be better off than to try and invent a new one. Seriously, though, forms are timeless. Look at pottery through the centuries, read books on art history, check out what others are doing. But, I do have some rules of thumb regarding form.

A good piece should feel as it looks—that is, its appearance should reflect its actual weight. For instance, a sturdy-looking bowl should have heft. And, visually, the maximum diameter of a turned bowl should never be in the center. It should divide a bowl horizontally into ⅖, ⅗, or ⅓, ⅔.

Another rule: The more colorful the wood, the more exciting the grain pattern, the simpler the form you need to show it off. However, that doesn't mean someone should neglect form altogether and rely on only the wood to make the bowl attractive. A good-looking bowl has to have the right balance.

---

proportionate dimensions, at least as preferred by the ancient Greeks. With the technique shown on the following pages, you'll be able to draw from an inventory of curves that open endless choices of form.

How to design with a chain

Proportioning a bowl's dimensions with the Golden Mean gives you the rough outline for your bowl-to-be. To find out the next step—how to come up with an attractive form—we called on Nancy Briggs, an experienced potter, artist, and photo stylist, who helps with project photography in *WOOD*® magazine's studio.

On the potter's wheel, Nancy has fashioned thousands of bowls, vases, cups, mugs, and platters. Form comes quite naturally to her. But, explaining how to create good form was another matter. Even after hours of research on the subject, Nancy could only report, "Nothing concrete." Then, we got our heads together and went over all the types of curves and arcs you'll find in bowls. What architects call a "catenary" intrigued us.

Bowl profile drawn with the aid of a hanging chain. Mahogany, 5¼×4".

Imagine a jewelry chain hanging freely around the neck. That's a catenary curve. Without tension, the chain forms a flowing, natural contour "perfect for the shape of a bowl," Nancy declared. She then offered to work on some variations.

Later, Nancy brought in a simple-to-do technique for designing bowl shapes. "It offers so many great possibilities that I plan to use it in designing some of my own work in clay," she said. "Besides, it's easy as well as fun to do."

continued

A SUREFIRE TECHNIQUE FOR PLEASING BOWL DESIGN

continued

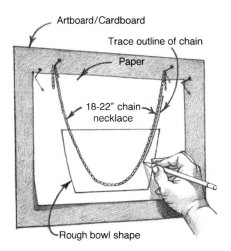

Artboard/Cardboard

Trace outline of chain

Paper

18-22″ chain necklace

Rough bowl shape

Begin by finding your bowl's basic proportions with the principle of the Golden Mean. Then, draw its full-sized, rough outline on a piece of paper. Now, tape a large piece of cardboard to a wall and fasten an 18–22" length of neck chain to it with a straight pin at both ends. The chain should drape without any tension.

To find a pleasing form for your bowl, slip the paper with the bowl outline behind the draped chain, then move the paper around. Change the shape of the chain's curve by repinning the ends. Try dipping the loop below the bowl's base outline and raising it above. The loop formed by the chain doesn't have to meet the base of your bowl. Experiment! Even turn your paper upside down to get convex shapes or tilt it to combine curves for more complex profiles.

When you've found the form you want to pursue, tape or pin the paper to the cardboard and track the chain's outline on your pattern with pinpricks through the links. Join the dots later with a continuous pencil line.

Nancy says that designing with this method not only sharpens your eye for form, but it's fun. The 13 different bowl profiles on these pages represent only a portion of the many she uncovered.

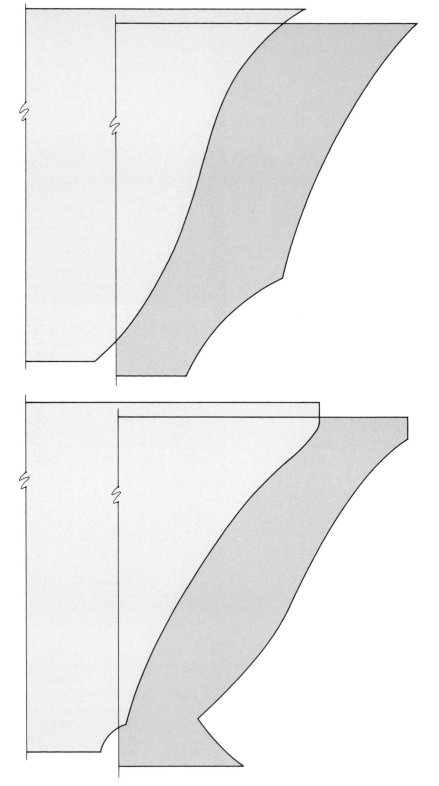

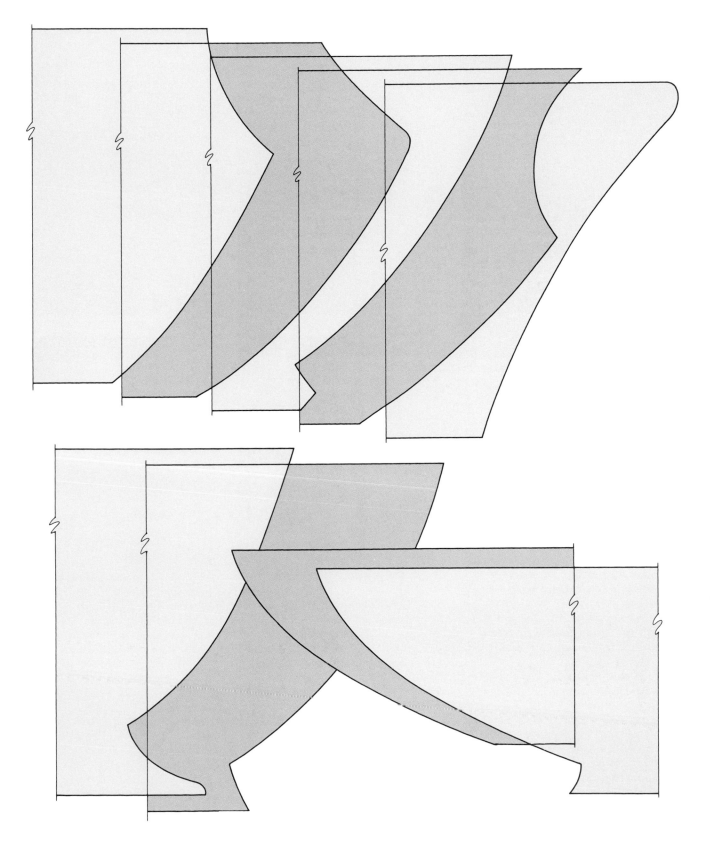

FACEPLATE TURNING

I t won't take long; we pro-
mise you that! Some people
get hooked on faceplate turning
the very first time they see a
beautifully crafted bowl quickly
take shape under the skillful
handling of their turning tools.
For others, the clincher comes
when they experience the thrill
of giving a one-of-a-kind project
to someone as a gift.

And you know something?
We've yet to meet a woodturner
who can find enough time to do
all the faceplate work he'd like
to do. That says something. If
you haven't had the pleasure
of spending some time with
turning tool in hand, you don't
know what you're missing.
There's no time like the present
to develop this great new habit.

Tools of the faceplate turning trade

No matter what the technique,
things always go more smoothly
when you have the right tool. And
faceplate work is no exception.
You could easily spend several
hundred dollars laying in all the
"right" tools, but we show a set of
six in the photo, *above right,* that
will get you off to a good start.

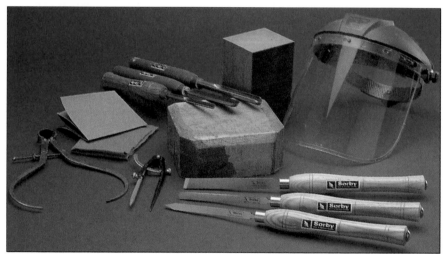

You should have three *gouges*—
two *spindle gouges* (a ¾" one and a
½" version) and a *bowl gouge*. The
spindle gouges make quick work of
rounding down the project as well as
shaping the outside of it. The flute of
the bowl gouge is much deeper than
the relatively shallow spindle gouges.
This shape allows you to remove
material from the inside of a project
without the tool's edges catching and
tearing the wood.

You'll also need a *parting tool,* a
round-nose scraper, and a *skew
chisel* in your arsenal. We've found
the parting tool quite helpful for

truing up the face of blanks,
roughing out the inside of end grain
projects, and in its normal role of
parting projects from the lathe. The
round-nose comes in handy in a
variety of situations, and we use the
skew chisel primarily for flattening
the inside bottom of bowls and
other flat-bottomed projects.

With a *compass* you can find the
approximate center of a blank and
establish the largest diameter of the
project. And a pair of outside
calipers allows you to check on the
progress of your turning from time
to time.

Sandpaper (80-, 120-, 150-, and 220-grit), a *face* shield to protect against flying shavings and dust, and a dust *mask* and *respirator* (not shown) for use while sanding and applying finishes round out the collection of necessities. Note the felt fabric beneath the sandpaper. We use it between the sandpaper and our fingers while sanding to prevent getting burned by the heat that results from the friction. Felt also allows the sandpaper to "fit" the contours of the turned shape.

Laying out your project

Most of us need to visualize the end product before we begin turning to ensure successful results. Here's our four-step strategy for deciding on the shape of the project and then transferring that shape to a template.

1. On a piece of tracing paper, draw a full-sized side view of the turning stock. Then, draw a perpendicular centerline through the side view. Now draw a trial shape on one side of the center line. If you don't like what you see, erase and repeat the procedure until you arrive at a pleasing shape. Allow space on all sides for getting the stock into round.

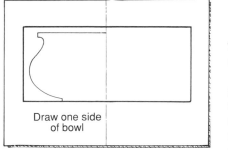
Draw one side of bowl

2. Fold the tracing paper on the centerline, and then trace the profile onto the other side of the line. Doing this will yield a symmetrical shape.

3. Unfold the tracing paper to view your handi-

Trace profile

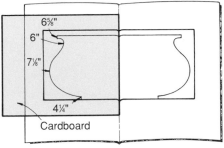
6⅝"
6"
7⅛"
4¼"
Cardboard

work. (We usually end up repeating the above process several times before we're satisfied.) Select the design that suits you best, then measure and mark the project's diameter at several high and low spots on your design. Doing this allows you to check your progress easily with calipers as you shape the project.

To make your template, glue card stock onto the back side of the tracing paper up to the centerline as shown *above*.

4. Finally, cut away the righthand portion of the tracing paper pattern and cut out the project's profile.

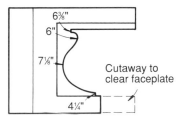
6⅜"
6"
7⅛"
4¼"
Cutaway to clear faceplate

Two good ways to mount stock on a lathe

Rather than confuse you by reciting the many ways to prepare the stock for turning, we've decided to show you two easy options, neither of which requires a commercial chuck.

The direct connect method. To reduce the possibility of the project breaking loose during turning, it's always best to secure the faceplate directly to the stock. Whether you can go this route, though, depends on whether or not there is enough extra material to accommodate the screws that must be driven into the stock.

1. Assuming that you do have sufficient material, start by finding the center of the blank by drawing

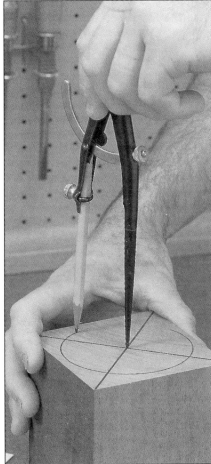

diagonals from corner to corner at each end of the stock. Then, mark the largest diameter needed for the project with a compass as shown in the photo *above*.

2. Now, plane or cut off the excess material at each corner of the blank. Doing this not only speeds the rounding-down process, but also, by removing off-center material, prevents the severe pounding a gouge takes when it repeatedly meets unfaceted corners. Swinging large amounts of off-center material exerts additional pressure on the bearings of your lathe, too. And when the bearings wear, the headstock typically exhibits some movement (or play), making it difficult for you to do quality work.

3. Center the faceplate over the center point that will face the headstock, and drill pilot holes for the screws that go into the blank;

continued

FACEPLATE TURNING
continued

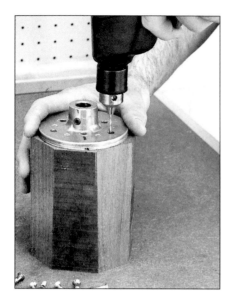

see photo *above*. (We use 1" flat-head brass wood screws as large in diameter as the holes in the face-plate. Why brass? If you hit one with a lathe tool, it's easier on the tool.)

4. Once you have driven the screws home, you can fasten the blank to the lathe.

The auxiliary faceplate method. When you just don't have enough material to allow you to screw the faceplate directly to the blank, you'll have to fashion an auxiliary faceplate and glue the stock to it. If you're working with a rough bowl blank, first smooth the surface that will contact the faceplate with a hand plane or a belt sander. This will ensure adequate adhesion between the auxiliary faceplate and the blank.

1. On the surface that will face the tailstock of the lathe (generally the open end of a project), mark the center point of the blank with a compass and scribe the largest desired diameter. Then, cut away the excess material, using the circumference line as a guide as shown in Photo A. Doing this gets rid of most off-center material before you mount the turning.

2. To make your auxiliary faceplate (it should be a bit larger

than the base of the finished turning), start by screwing the faceplate to a plywood or solid-wood scrap. Then, with a scrap of the correct size, scribe the circumference of the auxiliary faceplate as shown in Photo B. This automatically centers the faceplate on the auxiliary one.

3. Cut the excess material from the auxiliary faceplate, then screw the faceplate to the headstock of the lathe. Next, apply glue to the auxiliary faceplate as shown in Photo C, and adhere a piece of scrap notebook paper to it. This paper makes separating the finished project from the faceplate a snap.

4. Apply glue to the paper, move the tailstock up close to the headstock, and with the centerpoint of the blank in contact with the tailstock center, move the blank into contact with the auxiliary faceplate. "Clamp" the stock to the faceplate as shown in Photo D. This procedure self-centers the blank, which in turn, decreases off-center weight.

Note: This method works well when fastening face or edge grain to the auxiliary faceplate, but not when you have end grain facing the headstock. In the latter situation, the glue bond can't be counted on. Also, if you're working with green (unseasoned) wood, you'll have to use the direct-connect method or one of the chucks on the market.

Shaping the project

1. While no two faceplate turnings ever turn out the same way, they all begin with the rounding-down process. You do this to transform your out-of-round stock to a piece that's concentric to the drive shaft, which takes the stress off the machine. For the same reason, and for safety's sake, we've found it good practice to support the turning at both the head- and tailstock ends until

A

B

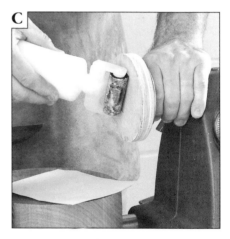

C

D

we've completely shaped the outside of the project.

2. In the photo immediately at *right* we've attempted to point out several things about rounding-down. First, notice the position of the tool rest. You want it as close to the blank as possible without actually touching it. Also note that it's a bit above the center of the project, though this can vary with the bevel angle of the tool you're using. And finally, take a look at the angle of the cutting edge to the blank. In actual practice, you position the bevel flat against the spinning stock, then raise the heel slightly so the cutting edge can do its job.

3. After rounding-down the blank, which we do at slow speed (400–600 rpm), true up the face of the project as shown in the photo at *right*. We have had good results attacking the face from the side and pushing straight across the face with a parting tool.

4. If you've had lots of experience turning projects, you can probably pull out your gouge and begin shaping the outside of the project, only occasionally referring to your template for direction. But we've found it helpful to lay the template on the blank as shown in Photo A, and transfer the marks on the template to the blank. Then we turn on the lathe (at medium speed 800–1,000 rpm), and use the parting tool to remove material at those points to the desired diameter. You'll want to check your progress occasionally with a pair of outside calipers as shown in Photo B. These incisions serve as reference points as you continue to shape the project.

5. As your project begins to take shape, check it often with the template as shown in Photo C. Hold the template perpendicular to the turning, and make marks at all points where the template and the blank make contact. Remove excess material where marked; don't do anything to areas you can see daylight between.

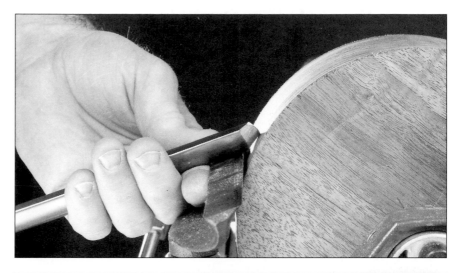

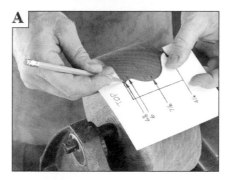

A

C

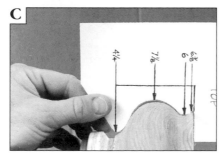

B

continued

FACEPLATE TURNING

continued

6. You can do most of the shaping work with the gouges, with some help from the bullnose and the parting tool. When you're satisfied with the outside shape, you may want to sand the project smooth. We go this route because the project still has full support at this point. We sand with a progression of garnet papers—80-, 120-, 150-, and 220-grit. Be sure to wear a dust mask or respirator while sanding, and keep the paper moving.

7. Shaping the inside of the project calls for a different set of tools and a few new procedures. Before hollowing out the project on the lathe, we remove the work from the headstock and drill a 1" hole in its center to the approximate depth we want the project's bottom to be. Use a drill-press setup like the one shown in Photo D. This hole not only serves as a reference point, but also seems to make the roughing-out process easier.

8. How you rough out the inside of the project depends on whether it's a face grain project or an end grain one. With the former, we use the deep-fluted bowl gouge as shown in Photo E. Notice that we work from the outside toward the center of the project. Note also the position of the gouge. It starts out on edge (with the toe doing the cutting), then as you work inward, you slowly rotate the gouge to a

more horizontal position. It may take a while to get the feel.

9. With end-grain projects, we rough out with a parting tool, again working toward the center hole—see Photo F. Note that we're

working at a slight angle to the workpiece.

10. The nearer you get to the outside edge of the project, the greater the tendency for the tool to want to "jump" to the outside. This

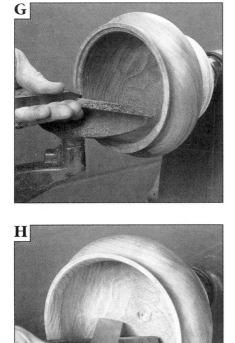

could require reshaping the lip, so we make starter cuts as shown in Photo G with a parting tool. This forms a ledge against which you can start the gouge.

11. You also can use the parting tool to establish the wall thickness. The wall thickness of bowls, goblets, and other projects should remain constant (we usually shoot for ¼" as a minimum). Periodically check your progress with the calipers.

12. To flatten the inside bottom of projects, we go with a skew chisel or a round-nose scraper. We "redesigned" the skew chisel shown in Photo H, rounding its cutting profile so that it won't catch the wood at the point where the walls and bottom meet.

Note: As you work the inside of your project, you may find it helpful to have a light source trained on the area being worked. Otherwise, the dust and shavings can quickly obstruct your vision.

Finishing up the project

1. One of the things most woodworkers like about lathe work is that they can rough out, shape, and finish a project while it's still on the lathe. We usually spend plenty of time sanding the project inside and out before finishing; when we hurry we regret it.

2. While sanding the project, you may notice some impossible-to-eradicate rough areas on the surface. If this happens, you may be time and effort ahead if you backtrack and very carefully cut away a bit more material, then resand. A properly sanded surface should almost shine.

3. When applying the finish, be sure you first protect the lathe bed and all nearby surroundings with newspapers. Otherwise, the spinning object can quickly make a mess of your shop.

4. In the two photos *above* and *above right* we show you how to separate the finished project from the lathe. If you employed the auxiliary face-plate method, first remove the faceplate from the auxiliary one. Then carefully tap a wood chisel, with the beveled edge facing the auxiliary faceplate, into

the paper joint line separating the project from the auxiliary faceplate until the bowl falls away. Then, sand the bottom smooth, and finish.

5. For those projects turned using the direct-connect mounting method, use your parting tool, with the lathe going at low speed (400–600 rpm) to separate the project from the remainder of the stock. Be sure to hold one hand beneath the project so you can catch it when the separation is complete.

6. If desired, you can sand and finish the bowl's bottom, and maybe carve your initials there, too.

A BEGINNER'S GUIDE TO TURNING WEED POTS

L ike most self-taught wood-turners, how-to editor Marlen Kemmet picked up his share of bad habits along the way. That's why he feels so fortunate to spend a day at the lathe with Rus Hurt, a profes-

Rus Hurt

sional turner who lives in Port Wing, Wisconsin. Rus, who has produced more than 2,000 weed pots during the past seven years, has developed a step-by-step turning method that anyone—including a beginner—can master. Following Rus's no-

nonsense procedure, Marlen now can turn out a blemish-free weed pot in less than 40 minutes. And after reading this article and turning a few practice pieces, you'll be able to do the same in no time at all.

Note: Sharp turning tools are a must. See "3 tools do the job" opposite for reference.

Turn your stock round

Note: If you don't have turning squares or dried firewood for your weed pot, see the Buying Guide for a source of turning squares.

1. Cut a piece of 3"- to 4"-square stock to 6" long. Draw diagonals on each end to find center.

2. Mount the stock between centers, using a spur center in the headstock end and a ball-bearing cup center in the tailstock.

3. With a ½" or ¾" gouge, turn the stock round as shown in Photo A. Bring the work into round with light cuts and a slow lathe speed of 600–800 rpm. As the piece becomes more cylindrical in shape, increase the speed to about 1,350 rpm, and take slightly heavier cuts. For stability and safety, stop the lathe and move the tool rest closer to the turning as you round down the stock.

A

Square both ends of the cylinder

1. Use a ⅛" parting tool to square the headstock end (the end that will become the base) and form a tenon as shown in Photo B. Turn the tenon to fit into the hole in your drill-press table. (We checked the diameter of the tenon with an outside calipers. If your drill-press table doesn't have a hole, drill a

B

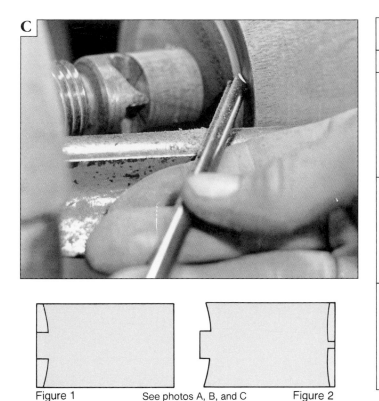

C

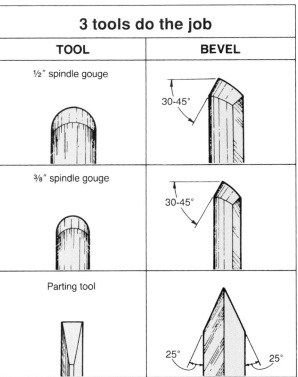

3 tools do the job

TOOL	BEVEL
½″ spindle gouge	30-45°
⅜″ spindle gouge	30-45°
Parting tool	25° 25°

Figure 1   See photos A, B, and C   Figure 2

¾" hole through a piece of ¾" plywood. Center the hole under the chuck, and fasten the plywood to your drill-press table to form an auxiliary table.) The tenon allows you to center and stabilize the turned blank flat on your drill-press table where shown in the drawing *right* titled Drilling the Throat Hole.

2. Using a ⅜" gouge, form a concave bottom (up to the tenon) on the turning as shown in Photo C and Figure 1 *above*. This shearing cut eliminates the torn end grain resulting from the scraping cuts made with the parting tool and results in much less sanding later. The concave bottom also helps the completed weed pot to sit level.

3. Repeat the previous two steps to form a ¼" tenon ¼" long on the opposite end of the turning and to create a concave surface where shown in Figure 2 *above*. For a tear-free surface near the throat hole, Rus prefers to make this tenon about ¹⁄₁₆" smaller than the diameter of the throat hole. This allows him to remove the entire tenon when drilling the throat hole.

4. Sand smooth the concave portion on the top of the turning. It's easier to sand this surface now,

before the tenon is removed. Remove the turning from the lathe.

Time to drill the throat hole

1. Chuck a ⁵⁄₁₆" brad-point bit into your drill press. Position the bottom tenon in the hole in your drill-press table or wooden auxiliary top. Then, center the point of the bit directly over the tailstock center indentation where shown in the drawing *right*.

2. With a drill-press speed of about 1,000 rpm, drill a ⁵⁄₁₆" hole as deep as possible into the turning where shown in the drawing. For larger weed pots, you may want to increase the diameter of the throat hole. To prevent the bit from overheating, Rus raises it several times and allows the spinning bit to clean the waste from the hole and bit.

3. To help recenter the throat-hole end of the turning on the cup center, form a countersink on the hole just drilled. To do this, stick the pointed end of a plumber's pipe reamer or large countersink in the throat hole and turn it by hand—usually about two revolutions of the reamer.

4. Remount the turning stock between centers.

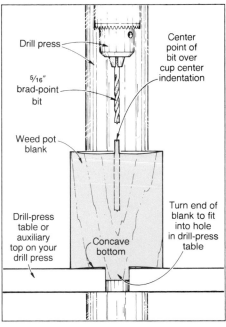

DRILLING THE THROAT HOLE

Turn the base to rough shape

1. Readjust the tool rest at an angle and close to the base of the turning for tool stability. See Photo D for reference. Hold a ⅜" spindle gouge in your left hand, and use your right hand to stabilize the tool *continued*

A BEGINNER'S GUIDE TO TURNING WEED POTS
continued

shaft on the tool rest. With the cutting tip of the gouge rolled slightly on its side and angled slightly upward, shape the arc for the base of the turning. See the drawing *opposite* titled Cuts to Form the Arc for reference on the sequence of cuts. Make continuous final cuts to create a smooth arc as shown in Photo D and Figure 3.

2. Readjust your tool rest, and start on the opposite side of line 1, making cuts toward the neck end (line 2) as shown in photo E and figure 4 to form the top of the base. To accomplish this, shift the tool to the right hand and stabilize the tool shaft on the tool rest with the left hand. After making the cuts to roughly shape the arc, make final continuous arced-cuts to create the smooth shape shown in Photo E.

Shape the neck
1. Start by making a reference cut at line 3 (the thinnest portion of the neck) with the parting tool. Cut until the diameter remaining is ¾" thick. (As shown in Photo F, we used outside calipers to ensure we didn't make the reference cut too deep.) See Figure 5 for reference before making the cut.

2. Start at the top of the previously formed base (line 2), and cut toward the neck reference cut. Then, with the gouge in your left hand and using your right hand for stabilizing the tool, begin the cut at the top of the turning, and turn to the neck reference cut as shown in Photo G. See Figure 6 for assistance.

3. Make light, curved cuts to finish shaping the neck as shown in Photo H and Figure 7.

Proportions: Rus's rule of thirds
To establish proportions for a weed pot, Rus suggests dividing the distance between the top and bottom (not including the tenons) into thirds. Then, he recommends marking reference lines on the cylinder where shown in the drawing at *right*. Line 1 (nearest the bottom) will be the widest proportion of the base. Line 2 is where the squatty base narrows for the neck. Mark a third line between line 2 and the top. This is where the neck will be at its narrowest. Remember, these are just guidelines; try slightly different shapes as shown at *right*.

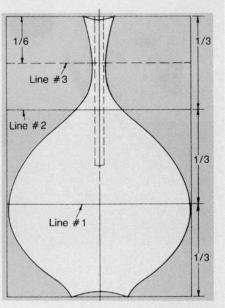

1/6 1/3
Line #3
Line #2
1/3
Line #1
1/3
1/3

D   E

Sand your weed pot smooth and apply the finish
1. Remove the tool rest from the lathe and slide the base to one side. Using progressively finer grits of sandpaper, ending with 400 grit, sand the weed pot smooth. (To

protect his fingers, Rus wraps the sandpaper around a foam rubber pad, and uses a lathe speed of 800 to 1,000 rpm.) For the final sanding, stop the lathe and sand with grain to prevent sanding rings from circling the finished weed pot.

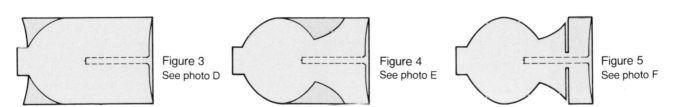

Figure 3
See photo D

Figure 4
See photo E

Figure 5
See photo F

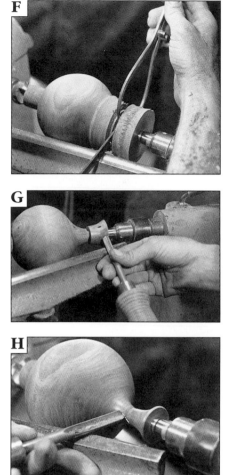

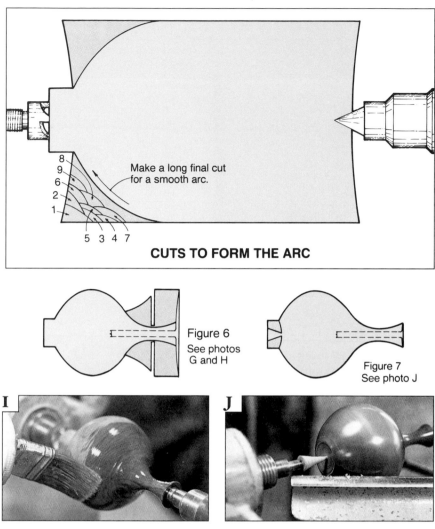

Make a long final cut for a smooth arc.

CUTS TO FORM THE ARC

Figure 6
See photos
G and H

Figure 7
See photo J

2. While slowly rotating the stock by hand, brush on the finish as shown in Photo I. Rus prefers Deft Clear Wood Finish (lacquer). Allow the finish to dry approximately 30 minutes.

3. Running the lathe at 800 to 1,000 rpm, lightly buff the finish with 0000 steel wool.

4. Wipe the surface with a clean cloth. (Often, Rus will dampen a cloth with Watco Satin Wax, to clean the turning. Then, he'll run the lathe, causing the liquid wax to evaporate quickly.)

5. Apply a coat of finish wax—any furniture wax with a high carnuba content will work—to the turning. To speed the drying, run the lathe for 30 seconds, and buff with a clean cotton cloth.

Parting the weed pot from the lathe

1. Using a ⅜" gouge, reduce the size of the tenon at the base. Turn the tenon to a cone shape as shown in Photo J and Figure 7.

2. Remove the turning from the lathe, and use a ¼" chisel to separate the tenon (don't snap it off as it may break fibers and leave an unsightly base). Sand the bottom of the weed pot. Sign and date the bottom of the weed pot, and then apply finish to the bottom.

Buying Guide

• **Turning squares**. For current prices of 4x4x12" pieces of walnut, maple, mahogany, and cherry, contact Constantine, 2050 Eastchester Road, Bronx, NY 10461, or call 800-223-8087.

Project Tool List
Lathe
    Spur drive center
    Revolving tail center
    ⅜", ½", ¾" spindle gouges
    Parting tool
Drill press
    ⁵⁄₁₆" bit

Note: *We built the project using the tools listed. You may be able to substitute other tools or equipment for listed items you don't have. Additional common hand tools and clamps may be required to complete the project.*

STACK-LAMINATED BOWLS

Borrowing a reader's technique for making stack-laminated bowls, we've turned some of the best-looking bowls to come out of the *WOOD*® magazine shop. With our step-by-step instructions, you can do the same even if you're a newcomer to woodturning. Then, sit back and watch your friends marvel at your latest accomplishment.

We've been dying to write this ever since we met woodworker and retired pilot Bill Lovelace in Phoenix. At the time, we were amazed by the looking-glass finish on his stack-laminated bowls. At $250–450 apiece, he sells every masterpiece he makes. As Bill says, "They're winners." And, we can't argue with that.

To let all of you in on Bill's secrets, we made another pilgrimage to his shop late last year. Then, we spent several days in our own shop, learning how to assemble and turn these exquisite bowls, and adding a few techniques of our own.

Not surprisingly, the process begins with planning the appearance of your bowl. Then, you build all the necessary layers and laminate them into a square blank. After you bandsaw the blank to a nearly round form, you mount it to your lathe and proceed to turn one gem of a bowl, complete with shiny facets of various-colored woods.

Just keep this bit of advice in mind: When your lathe screams "uncle" from turning so many of these bowls, give it a short break while you assemble another one.

Planning: Like making cutting boards

1. If you've ever assembled a cutting board of your own design, you've already made many of the same types of decisions that go into planning a stack-laminated bowl. First of all, determine the size (diameter and height) of your bowl by considering its use (decorative or functional) and placement in your home. Bill Lovelace turns only 12"-diameter bowls because, as he says, "people love big bowls—they sell great."

2. Just as you have a lot of flexibility in the size of a bowl or

SOME INTERESTING POSSIBILITIES

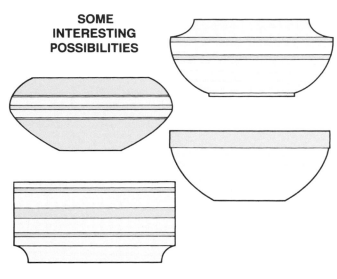

Determining width of bowl-blank segments

Bowl Dia.	Profile thickness						
	¼"	⅝"	1"	1½"	2"	2¼"	3"
4"	1"	1¼"	1½"	1¾"			
6"	1¼"	1½"	1¾"	2¼"	2½"	2¾"	
8"	1½"	1¾"	2¼"	2½"	2¾"	3¼"	3¼"
10"	1¾"	2¼"	2½"	2¾"	3¼"	3½"	4"
12"	2¼"	2½"	2¾"	3¼"	3½"	4"	4½"

To determine the width of your bowl-blank segments, find the figure in the chart that corresponds to the diameter and profile thickness of your bowl design.

cutting board, you also can choose any profile or laminate design for your bowl. To give you an idea of the possibilities, Design Editor Jim Downing drew up a few options shown *above*.

3. Once you've decided on the bowl's look, it's time to determine the thickness of the bowl's profile.

4. First, draw a side profile (see three examples *right*). Then, measure the thickness of the profile and refer to the chart on the next page to determine the width of the bowl blank segments. As shown in the top view of bowl blank layers *right*, every layer above the bottom layer consists of two long segments of equal size and two equally sized short segments. The length of the long segments equals the diameter of your bowl. When you place the short segments between the long segments, the short segments should be long enough to form a square layer.

Cut, clamp, and stack: Making simple layers

1. Simple layers, such as the bottom three and top two tiers in the photo *opposite,* have one wood species, with edge-to-end joints, and only five segments for the bottom layer and four segments for the other laminates. Feature layers, such as the one shown third from the top in the photo *opposite,* may consist of several types of wood, with face-to-face, face-to-edge, edge-to-end, and edge-to-edge joints, and an unlimited number of wood pieces in several species. We'll talk about feature layers later.

2. Before cutting any stock, use a square to set your tablesaw blade to exactly 90°. This step, more than any other, will lead to the tight joints that distinguish a great bowl from a so-so effort. Also, to ensure tight joints between layers, plane all the stock for each layer to the same thickness before making any cuts. Don't be in a rush as you cut the parts—your patience will lead to segments with flat, perpendicular surfaces and crisp corners—key ingredients for tight joints.

A handy device for quick clamping

To take some of the hassle out of clamping, we suggest you build the

platform shown on *page 53* from polyester or melamine-coated particleboard. This "lily pad," or "toadstool" as it came to be known around our shop, provides an elevated surface that dried glue and laminated segments easily separate

continued

PROFILE THICKNESS

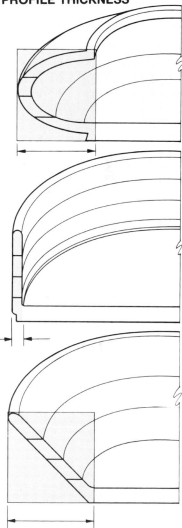

TOP VIEW OF BOWL BLANK LAYER

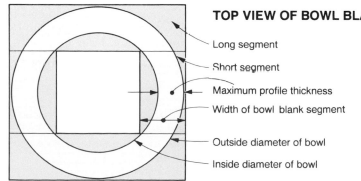

Long segment

Short segment

Maximum profile thickness

Width of bowl blank segment

Outside diameter of bowl

Inside diameter of bowl

51

STACK-LAMINATED BOWLS
continued

from without waxed paper. For all the gluing operations, you can make perfectly flat layers by clamping segments between the toadstool and another piece of coated particleboard. A 4X8' sheet of this material costs about $40 at lumberyards. If you want to avoid this expense, clamp your layers between waxed paper and particleboard. We suggest you make at least one platform; and if you want to work fast, you'll use as many as three at once.

Let's build the bowl

1. With the steps on the *previous page* done, it's time to get to the fun part—assembling your bowl. Starting at the bottom and working up, use yellow woodworker's glue to join the three bottom segments as shown in Photo A.

2. Now, clamp them together as shown in Clamping Setup 1 *opposite*. No matter how straight you try to line up these pieces, they won't set flush enough to form a tight joint to adjacent long segments, as shown in Photo B. To solve this problem, pass one side through your tablesaw as shown in Photo C, taking off just enough to straighten that side (usually not more than ⅛"). Now, flip the segment over and do the same for the other side.

3. Once you've squared-up this piece, glue and clamp it to two

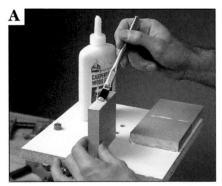

Spread liberal amounts of glue on both surfaces wherever you join two pieces. Here, we're gluing the middle segment of the bowl's bottom.

Since its nearly impossible to glue the middle segment of the bowl's bottom perfectly straight...

...take off a minimum amount of stock on both sides with your tablesaw to square the segment.

To hold the layers in place while you sand them, lay them on a sheet of sandpaper attached to your bench with double-faced tape.

longer segments to form the bowl bottom as shown in Clamping Setup 2 *opposite*. After this layer dries, use a finishing sander with 60-grit paper as shown in Photo D to smooth out the surface. Remove a minimum of stock and don't gouge the wood. Now, assemble

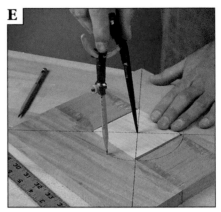

Use a scrap block and compass to draw the circular cutaway hole in the center of each layer. This makes for easier turning later.

the remaining layers as shown in Clamping Setup 3 *opposite*. Sand these layers smooth just as you did the bottom.

4. After these layers dry, round-out their center hole for ease of turning later. To do this, make a scrap block just big enough to fit in the hole. With the scrap block in the hole, find its center by drawing two lines connecting opposite corners of the layer—their intersection marks the center. Use a compass as shown in Photo E to draw a circular center. Remove the scrap block and cut along this line with either a scrollsaw or jigsaw.

5. If you're not interested in making a bowl with a feature layer, jump ahead to the section "Preparing the Blank for Turning" on *page 54*.

Feature Layers: Not all that complicated

1. You can try almost anything design-wise when making feature layers, just remember these guidelines: Although made of many more pieces, feature layers still consist of two long and two short segments, just like the other layers. The only difference: Several pieces make up these assemblies. The four segments should match the width

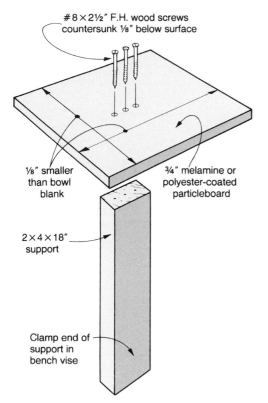

#8 × 2½" F.H. wood screws countersunk ⅛" below surface

⅛" smaller than bowl blank

¾" melamine or polyester-coated particleboard

2 × 4 × 18" support

Clamp end of support in bench vise

and length of the long and short segments of the other layers.

If one of the segments has horizontal pieces, such as the one in our sample feature layer shown *below right,* the thickness of that segment determines the thickness of the layer. For example, the bowl on *page 50* has a feature layer with two pieces of ¾"-thick stock and one piece of ¼"-thick stock, making for a 1¾"-thick feature layer.

2. After you determine the width and length of the four segments in the feature layer, cut all the pieces for them ½" too long and ½" too wide. This extra stock allows you to square the pieces later by trimming them to finished size. To clamp these segments, follow Clamping Setup 4 *above right.* Note that we placed a ⅛" dowel under one piece so it can serve later as a ripping guide.

continued

CLAMPING SETUPS

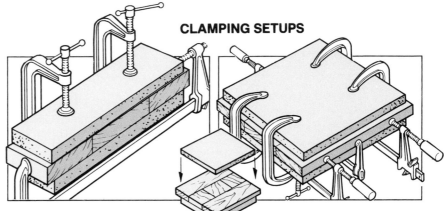

1. Use this Clamping Setup to join the 3 pieces that make up the middle segment in the bottom layer. Allow to dry at least 15 minutes.

2. To join the two long segments and laminated middle segment of the bottom layer, first lightly tighten the four small clamps over the joint lines.

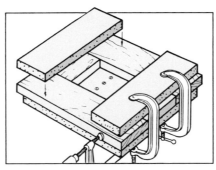

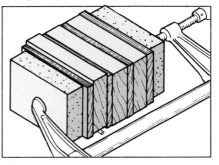

3. For layers other than the bottom, first place two clamps over the joint lines, then join all the segments with two longer clamps.

4. Place a ⅛" dowel under one piece when you clamp a complex segment. The raised piece provides a straight edge when you trim the segment.

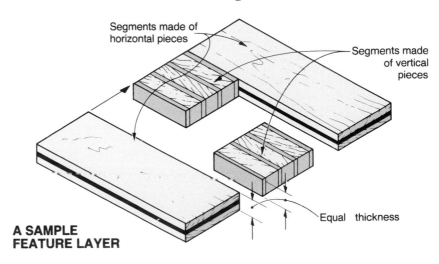

Segments made of horizontal pieces

Segments made of vertical pieces

Equal thickness

A SAMPLE FEATURE LAYER

STACK-LAMINATED BOWLS
continued

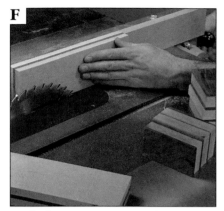

With the power OFF, set the rip fence to the height of one segment, test the setting with a scrap piece, and then. . .

. . . pass the other segments through the blade. We're using a pushstick and abrasive belt cleaner to safely hold the segment.

We used waxed ¼" dowels as guide-pins and lowered the successive layers on them as we glued. We sanded the ends of the dowels to round them off.

3. For our example, we cut the segments made of vertical pieces to the right thickness by setting our rip fence as shown in Photo F. To do this yourself, snugly squeeze the segment composed of horizontal pieces between the blade and fence. Lock the fence there and remove the segment. Now, cut a scrap piece and check your accuracy by comparing the thickness of the scrap stock and the horizontal-piece segment on a flat surface such as the table of your saw. Repeat this process until the thickness of the pieces matches. In Photo G, we show you how to safely saw short segments to match the thickness of the long segment. Finally, glue, clamp, sand, and cut out a circular center for this layer as you did for the others.

Preparing the blank for turning

1. Once you've finished the layers, dry-stack them together in their finished order. For appearance and strength, stack them just as you would lay bricks, with as little joint alignment as

possible. For example, note how we alternated the position of the layers in the photo on *page 50*. After you're satisfied with the alignment, dry-clamp the layers and drill holes for guidepins in two opposite corners. You want the pins (nails or waxed dowels) to fit snugly. Then, draw a line down the height of any side of the stack as a reference mark for reassembling the layers during gluing.

2. Next, unclamp the stack and place the guidepins in the bottom layer. Working fast, apply glue to both sides of the joining layers and stack them one by one on top of another as shown in Photo H. If you don't feel you can assemble the blank in 15 minutes, switch to a slower-drying white woodworker's glue. When you're finished gluing, put a sheet of coated particleboard over the stack and clamp it together, spacing the clamps 2" apart around the blank. For a solid lamination that won't come apart on the lathe or separate at the joint lines after finishing, allow this assembly to dry overnight (at least eight hours).

3. Next, determine the center of the bottom of the blank with two intersecting lines just as you did for each layer. With a compass centered on the bottom, draw a circle as large as possible without going off the side of the blank. Finally, follow this line with your bandsaw to make the blank round.

4. To get your bowl mounted on the lathe, we recommend using a hardwood or Baltic birch auxiliary faceplate at least one-half the diameter of your bowl blank. To apply the auxiliary faceplate, draw a centered circle on the bottom of the bowl that's the diameter of your auxiliary faceplate and apply as shown in Photo I.

How the stacked bowl turns

By now, you've probably invested 15–30 hours in constructing your bowl, so you don't want to botch the turning job. Because of the likelihood of chip-out along the joint lines, and the many directions that the grain runs, turning these bowls poses special problems. As Design Editor Jim

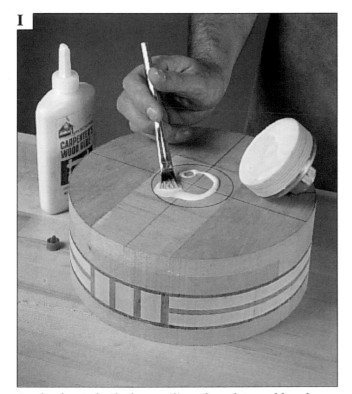

I

Apply glue to both the auxiliary faceplate and bowl-blank bottom. You also can use 5-minute epoxy to speed this process and spare the clamping.

J

You can sand the bowl by hand, but you'll save yourself a lot of time by power-sanding. An angle drill works well on the inside wall of the bowl.

Downing puts it, "Cutting against the grain is like petting your dog from his tail to his head—in the same way, your turning tools will ruffle the grain just as your hand ruffles his hair." Here's how to avoid these problems or handle them as they occur:

First, start with a sharp set of tools and keep them sharp as you go. Now, set your lathe for 500–600 rpm, and rough the outside of the bowl round with a round-nose scraper. Next, do the same for the inside.

Increase the lathe speed to 900–1,000 rpm, and use the round-nose scraper to shape the outside profile. With the same scraper, slowly and carefully scrape the inside profile, keeping the wall ½" thick (you'll sand away ¼" later, finishing with a ¼"-thick bowl). If you try to remove too much wood quickly on the inside, your tool will catch on the stock, gouging your bowl.

Now, use a skew chisel to smooth the outside walls and inside base of the bowl. Smooth the inside with a round-nose scraper— we found that ½" tools catch less frequently than larger scrapers. Again, go slowly on both the outside and inside to minimize grain tear-out, and you'll save yourself some sanding later.

To speed up sanding, use a power drill and a 50-grit sanding disc to power-sand the inside bottom and outside walls of the bowl while it's turning at 900–1,000 rpm as shown in Photo J. Unless you have an angle drill, you'll have to sand the inside walls by hand. After you've removed all the tear-out, sand the bowl through a succession of grits. Finish the bowl with sanding sealer and polyurethane or lacquer while it's on the lathe.

TURNING PROJECTS

Turn out a host of great gift items with the projects we offer here.
You'll find candle stick holders, napkin rings, and holiday
decorations that are sure to delight friends and family alike.

MASTERPIECE MUSIC BOX

This lathe-turned music box will strike a responsive chord with anybody who appreciates beautiful wooden objects—we guarantee it! And even with the rich-looking veneer inlays that accent its traditional lines, you'll waltz right through this project, completing it in just a few enjoyable hours.

1. Trace or draw the full-sized bottom pattern *below* onto a 1/4x4x12" piece of walnut. Back the workpiece with scrapwood, and bore a 3/16"-deep counterbore where shown with a 1 1/8" Forstner bit or spade bit chucked into a drill press. Change to a 3/8" brad-point bit, and drill through the center of the counterbore.

2. With a 1/4" brad-point bit in the drill press, drill the center hole and six 1/8"-deep counterbores where shown. Then, drill 1/8" holes through the six counterbores.

3. Cut out the bottom with a bandsaw or scrollsaw. Sand, and apply a clear oil finish to both sides. Mount the musical movement on the flat side with the winding stem protruding through the 3/8" hole, and then set the bottom aside.

Start turning on the inside

1. Glue a piece of scrapwood 1 1/2x4 1/2x4 1/2" to the face of the turning blank that will be the top of your music box. This will become your auxiliary faceplate. Clamp until dry, and then draw diagonal lines on the scrapwood faceplate.

2. Using the junction of the lines as a center, scribe one circle 4 1/2" in diameter and another one the same diameter as your 3–4" lathe faceplate. Bandsaw around the outside line. Then, place your lathe faceplate inside the smaller circle, and screw it to the auxiliary faceplate.

3. True the side of the blank with your gouge. Then, place the tool rest parallel to the face, true the face, and locate the center on it. To do this, move a pencil point across the rotating workpiece until it marks a point, not a circle.

4. From the centerpoint, mark two circles, one 2 3/8" in diameter (1 3/16" radius) and one 3 1/4" (1 5/8" radius). With your 3/8" gouge, turn a 1 1/2"-deep hole inside the smaller circle (see the Turning the Opening drawing, on *page 58)*. You don't need to sand this recess. Since the music-box movement fits into it, it won't be visible.

5. Inside the larger circle, cut a recess 5/8" deep with your gouge. Test-fit the bottom with the music box mounted on it, adjusting the size of the two openings, if necessary. The wall of the larger hole will show after assembly, so sand it with 100-, 150-, 220-, 320-, and 400-grit sandpaper.

6. Next, transfer the full-sized template to a piece of stiff cardboard, and turn the side profile. With your parting tool, cut the 3/8"-wide groove for the inlay 1/8" deep. Check the width against the inlay as you work.

Form a tenon to turn the top

1. Part off the body at the glue joint. Then, form a tenon on the auxiliary faceplate to fit the large

continued

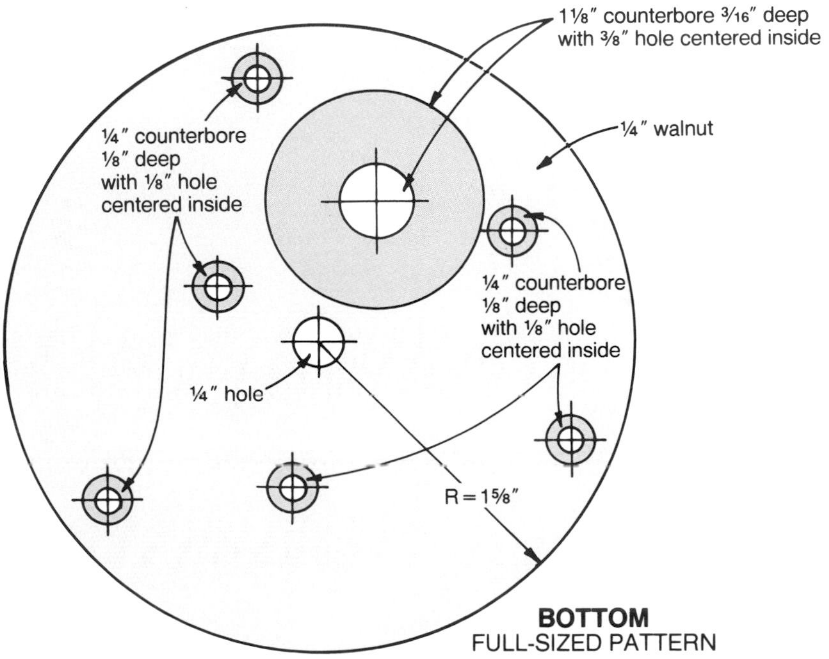
1 1/8" counterbore 3/16" deep
with 3/8" hole centered inside
1/4" counterbore
1/8" deep
with 1/8" hole
centered inside
1/4" walnut
1/4" counterbore
1/8" deep
with 1/8" hole
centered inside
1/4" hole
R = 1 5/8"

BOTTOM
FULL-SIZED PATTERN

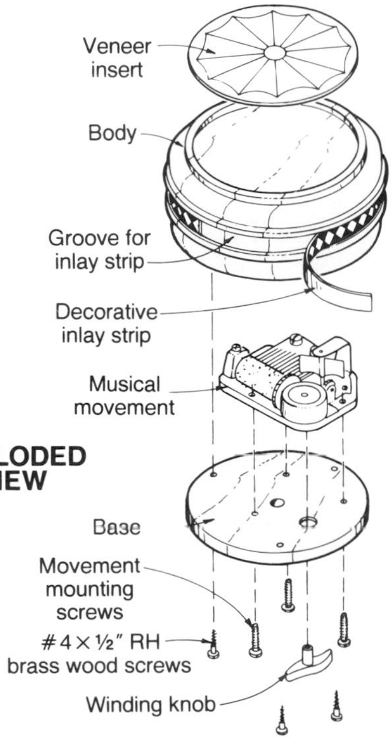
Veneer insert
Body
Groove for inlay strip
Decorative inlay strip
Musical movement
Base
Movement mounting screws
#4 x 1/2" RH brass wood screws
Winding knob

EXPLODED VIEW

MASTERPIECE MUSIC BOX
continued

recess in the turning (see the Turning the Top drawing, *below)*. With the body mounted snugly on the tenon, turn the face down to achieve an overall body height of 1¾".

2. Locate the center on the top face, and then mark a 3"-diameter circle on it for the inlay relief. (Measure your round veneer insert to make sure of the size.) Cut the relief ⁵⁄₃₂" deep. The wood in the middle will be less than ⅛" thick as you reach that depth, so make your cuts carefully. Sand the body, except for the inlay areas, with progressively finer sandpaper from 100- to 400-grit.

Dress it up with veneers

1. Apply a thin layer of glue to the back of the inlay strip. Then, starting from one end, press it into the groove. Cut off the overlapping end with an X-acto knife. Secure the inlay with a heavy rubber band, and then wipe away excess glue.

2. Carefully remove the circular inlay from the carrier by cutting the paper tape with an X-acto knife. Apply glue to the wood side of the inlay, position it, and clamp by pressing a scrapwood circle against it with your lathe's tailstock.

3. When the glue is dry, remove the body from the lathe. Carefully remove the paper tape by moistening a small area with a damp rag and scraping the tape away. Do not wet the inlay excessively. Handsand the veneer inlays, and then apply a clear oil finish to the music box, inside and outside. Using the bottom piece as a template, drill ¹⁄₁₆" pilot holes into the music-box body. Finally, attach the bottom with three #4x½" roundhead brass wood screws.

Supplies
Stock: Walnut bowl-turning blank, 2x4½x4½"; Walnut stock, ¼x4x12" Lathe tools: 3–4" faceplate with a 4½"-diameter auxiliary faceplate; ⅜" gouge, ⅛" parting tool.

Lathe speeds
Roughing: 600–900 rpm; Finishing and sanding: 1,200–1,500 rpm.

Buying Guide
• **Inlays and movement.** Inlay strip for side, style No. B17, round inlay for top, No. IW845, and Swiss musical movement (Brahm's "Lullaby," MUS3). Kit No. WD892. For current prices, contact Constantine's, 2050 Eastchester Road, Bronx, NY 10461, or call 800-223-8087.

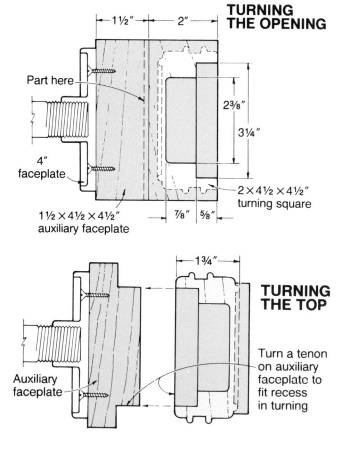

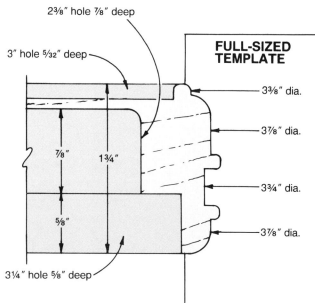

TURN SCRAPS INTO PINCUSHIONS

Whether new to wood-turning or an old lathe hand, you'll get a kick out of these practical pincushions that you can turn in a hurry from little scraps of wood. We'll get you started with easy instructions and a pair of patterns, but we'll bet you'll soon try some designs of your own.

1. Photocopy the template of your choice, *below right,* and transfer it to card stock, such as an index card. Mark the center on a scrapwood auxiliary faceplate, and then screw it to a 3" lathe faceplate.

2. Glue the turning stock to the center of the auxiliary plate with woodworker's glue or, for a faster start-up, cyanoacrylate adhesive. When the glue has dried, mount the faceplate on the lathe and bring the tailstock with a cone center up to the workpiece.

3. Now, with your gouge, round your turning stock down to the largest diameter shown for the pattern you've chosen. True the top edge (the tailstock end) and define the bottom of the base with a ⅛" parting tool. Cut in about ½" at the bottom, pointing the tool slightly toward the top of the turning for a concave base.

4. Turn the outside, forming the coves with either a ¼" round-nose or a gouge. Sand with 100-, 150-, 220-, and 400-grit paper.

Next, slide the tailstock back and bring the tool rest around to the end of the turning. Hollow out the top of the cup with your gouge, forming a rounded recess about ¾–1" deep. You won't need to sand inside since it will be covered. For ease of handling, apply a clear finish with the turning still attached to the faceplate. Part from the lathe, and sand and finish the bottom.

5. For the cushion, cut a circle of velvet about twice the diameter of the cup opening. Lay it face down, and then place a ball of polyester fill or 0000 steel wool on the center of the cloth. Gather the edge, and stitch it closed. Glue the cushion into place with cyanoacrylate adhesive.

Supplies
Stock: Miscellaneous scraps of turning stock, about 3×3×6".
Lathe tools: 3" faceplate with scrapwood auxiliary faceplate,

tailstock cone center, ⅜" gouge, ¼" roundnose, ⅛" parting tool.
Lathe speeds
Roughing, 600–900 rpm; finishing and sanding, 1,200–1,500 rpm.

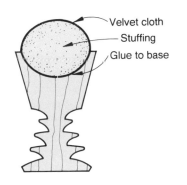

- Velvet cloth
- Stuffing
- Glue to base

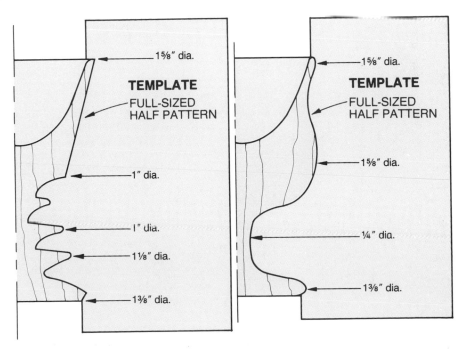

TEMPLATE
FULL-SIZED HALF PATTERN

1⅝" dia.

1" dia.

1" dia.

1⅛" dia.

1⅜" dia.

TEMPLATE
FULL-SIZED HALF PATTERN

1⅝" dia.

1⅝" dia.

¼" dia.

1⅜" dia.

DECORATOR OIL LAMPS

These turned, tuliplike lamps add a cheerful touch to any setting, any time. But they really shine when you light them. Then, their warm glow lends a delightful air to any occasion.

1. You can turn the three parts that make up the lamp from the same wood, or choose contrasting woods for the striking effect shown in the photo at *left.* (We used maple and walnut.) Turn the lamp holder from a 2½ x 2½ x 7½" square. Draw diagonals to locate the center on each end. With a brad-point bit and a drill press, drill a centered ⅛" hole 2" deep at one end.

2. Mount the square with a screw center at the headstock and a cone center at the tailstock (the drilled end goes at the tailstock). Transfer the templates, *opposite,* to light cardboard and cut them out.

3. Leaving about ½" of square stock at the headstock end, round down the turning with a ½" gouge. With your parting tool, cut in to ½" diameter 1⅜" headstock and ¾" diameter 1⅝" from the tailstock. Form the supporting cones, and then turn the lamp holder to the template dimensions. Sand with progressively finer grits from 150 to 400 before parting off the waste at the tailstock end where shown on the Forming the Lamp Holder drawing,

Step 1, *opposite.* Remove the turning from the screw center.

Drilling for the oil lamp
1. Grip the square bottom with a handscrew clamp, and drill an ¹¹⁄₁₆" hole for the Pyrex lamp insert, centering it on the ⅛" hole. Next, turn the workpiece end for end, placing the flat top on the drill-press table. Wrap a shop rag around the turning. Then, grip it with a handscrew clamp, and drill a ⅜" hole 2⅛" deep (⁹⁄₁₆" into the holder bottom) where shown on the Forming the Lamp Holder drawing, Step 2. Saw the waste off and sand the bottom.

A spindle for a stem
1. Working your way down the lamp, locate and mark the center on each end of a 1 x 1" square 8" long. Remove the screw center from your lathe and install a spur center to turn the stem.

2. After rounding down the stock, mark the turning sections from your template. Then, cut the coves with your spindle gouge. Roll the center beads with a gouge or skew, checking the contour with the template. Form a ⅜" tenon ½" long on each end. Sand, and then remove the stem from the lathe.

Finish up with the faceplate
1. Turn the base from ⅞"-thick stock 3½" square. Cover your 3" faceplate surface with double-faced tape, stick the wood to it, and clamp for about 20 minutes.

2. With the base template as a guide, shape and sand the base, and mark the center for the stem hole. Hold the faceplate with a handscrew clamp as you bore the ⅜" hole ⁹⁄₁₆" deep with a brad-point bit in a drill press. Now, remove the base turning from the faceplate—dribble lacquer thinner along the joint to break the bond.

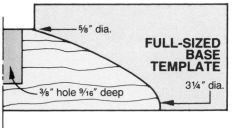

FULL-SIZED BASE TEMPLATE

5/8″ dia.

3/8″ hole 9/16″ deep

3¼″ dia.

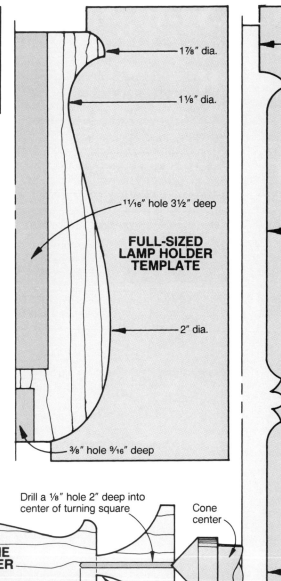

FULL-SIZED LAMP HOLDER TEMPLATE

1⅞″ dia.

1⅛″ dia.

11/16″ hole 3½″ deep

2″ dia.

3/8″ hole 9/16″ deep

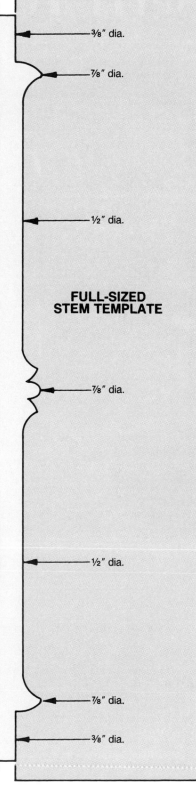

FULL-SIZED STEM TEMPLATE

3/8″ dia.

7/8″ dia.

½″ dia.

7/8″ dia.

½″ dia.

7/8″ dia.

3/8″ dia.

3. Assemble the lamps with woodworking glue. After applying a clear finish, install the lamp inserts, pour in some lamp oil, and light them up to cast a warm glow over the scene.

Supplies
Screw center; spur center; cone tail center; 3″ faceplate
Stock: 2½ × 2½ × 7½″ maple; 1×1×8″, ⅞×3½×3½″ walnut
Lathe tools: ½″ spindle gouge, ½″ skew, ⅛″ parting tool

Buying Guide
• **Lamp inserts.** Two Pyrex glass inserts with wicks. For current prices, contact Warren Vienneau, 146 Ridge Ave., Pittsfield, MA 01201, or call 413-443-2907.

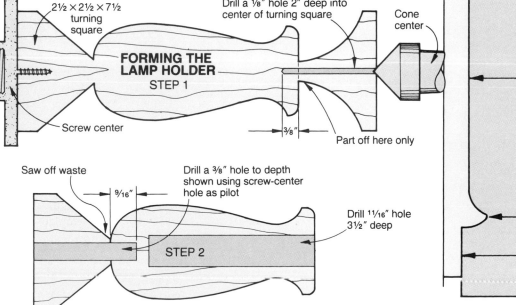

2½ × 2½ × 7½ turning square

Drill a ⅛″ hole 2″ deep into center of turning square

Cone center

FORMING THE LAMP HOLDER
STEP 1

Screw center

Part off here only

3/8″

Saw off waste

Drill a 3/8″ hole to depth shown using screw-center hole as pilot

9/16″

Drill 11/16″ hole 3½″ deep

STEP 2

SPLIT-TURNED VASE

Bob Taylor developed an early appetite for turning. At age 5, he was ready to start turning but unable to reach the lathe. To solve the problem, his father, an industrial arts teacher, built him a box to stand on. Bob, now a professor at Auburn University, still enjoys lathe work in his spare time. In fact, this split-vase design is one of his better sellers at craft fairs.

Note: You'll need two 2X2X24" turning squares to make this project. If you don't have stock this size, laminate thinner stock or see the Buying Guide on page 64 for our source.

Preparing the stock for turning

1. Cut four pieces of 2x2" stock (we used oak) to 11¾" long.

2. Joint two *adjacent* edges of each piece; check that the jointed edges are square to each other.

3. Now, rip the *other two edges* of each piece so each piece measures 1⅞" square.

4. Cut two pieces of heavy paper (we used a grocery sack) to 2" wide by 10¾" long.

5. Glue and clamp two of the turning squares with the paper in place where shown in Step 1 of the drawing *below left.* Please note the end-grain configuration. Check that the edges and ends are flush. Later, use an X-acto knife to trim the excess paper. The paper allows the lamination to be split after turning. Repeat with the other two squares.

6. Cut one piece of the paper to 3⅜" wide by 10¾" long. Glue and clamp the two laminations.

7. To support the corners—they have a tendency to chip when turning—wrap 1" strapping tape around the lamination where shown on Step 2 of the drawing.

8. Transfer the full-sized Template patterns on *page 64* to posterboard, and cut them to shape.

It's time to shape the inside

1. Using Step 2 of the drawing for reference, and the *inside template* on *page 64*, turn the lamination to shape. (We recommend a lathe speed of 750

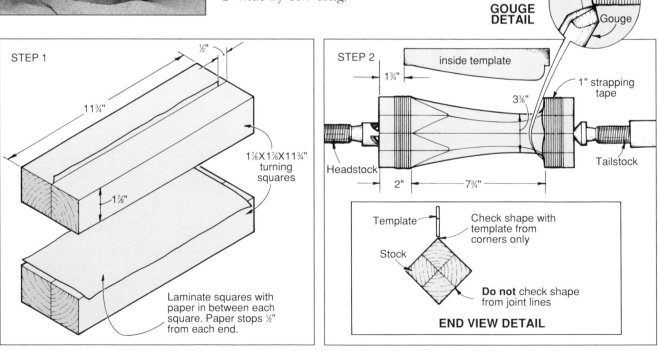

STEP 1

½"

11¾"

1⅞"

1⅞"X1⅞"X11¾" turning squares

Laminate squares with paper in between each square. Paper stops ½" from each end.

STEP 2

GOUGE DETAIL

Gouge

inside template

1¾"

3⅜"

1" strapping tape

Headstock

Tailstock

2"

7¾"

Template

Check shape with template from corners only

Stock

Do not check shape from joint lines

END VIEW DETAIL

rpm. To minimize chipping, we used a sharp ½" gouge.) Avoid using a scraper; it tends to leave a rough surface. Also, to reduce chipping at the radiused end, see the Gouge detail for tool-positioning reference when making the cut. Stop frequently and check the shape of the curve against that of the inside template where shown on the End View detail accompanying Step 2 of the drawing. *Don't make the curve too deep. The deeper the curve, the larger the openings in the completed vase.*

2. Sand the curved area smooth. Remove the strapping tape and split the lamination as shown in the photo at *right.*

Turn the outside to shape

1. Glue and clamp (no paper this time) the four turning squares in the positions shown on Step 3 of the drawing. Make sure that the curves stay aligned with each other when clamping. Let the glue dry overnight.

2. Using the *outside template* and a gouge, turn the vase lamination to the shape shown in Step 4 of the drawing. (We used a speed of about 1,200 to 1,500 rpm to minimize tool chatter caused by the openings.) Leave a ¾"-diameter waste tenon on the top and on the bottom of the turning.

continued

Using a mallet and 1" chisel, split the lamination at the four paper joints.

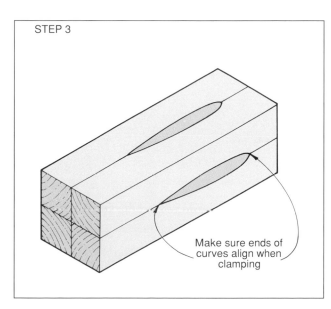

STEP 3

Make sure ends of curves align when clamping

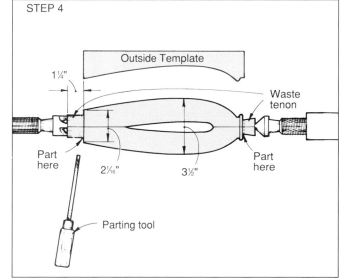

STEP 4

Outside Template

1¼"

Waste tenon

Part here

Part here

2¹⁄₁₆"

3½"

Parting tool

63

SPLIT-TURNED VASE
continued

3. Remove the tool rest and sand the vase. (We wrapped sandpaper around a felt pad to do this.) Holding your hand under the turning—like you'd throw a slow-pitch softball—sand the turning. *Don't* wrap your thumb around to the top of the turning. Holding the paper underneath the turning and using a speed of about 1,200 rpm helps prevent the sandpaper from catching in the openings.

4. Alternating between the top and base, make parting cuts at each tenon where shown on Step 4 of the drawing. Angle the tool where shown so the vase bottom is slightly concave and will sit flat. Do the same with the top to create the angled opening.

5. Remove the turning from the lathe and use a ⅝" Forstner bit to bore a hole through the top of the turning and into the hollow middle. Sand the top of the bored opening smooth. Apply finish.

Buying Guide
• **Turning squares.** 2 pieces of 2×2×24" red oak, catalog no. WD291. For current prices, contact Constantine's, 2050 Eastchester Rd., Bronx, NY 10461, or call 800-223-8087.

Project Tool List
Tablesaw
Jointer
Drill press
  ⅝" bit
Lathe
  Spur drive center
  Cone center
  ½" spindle gouge
  Parting tool

Note: We built the project using the tools listed. You may be able to substitute other tools or equipment for listed items you don't have. Additional common hand tools and clamps may be required to complete the project.

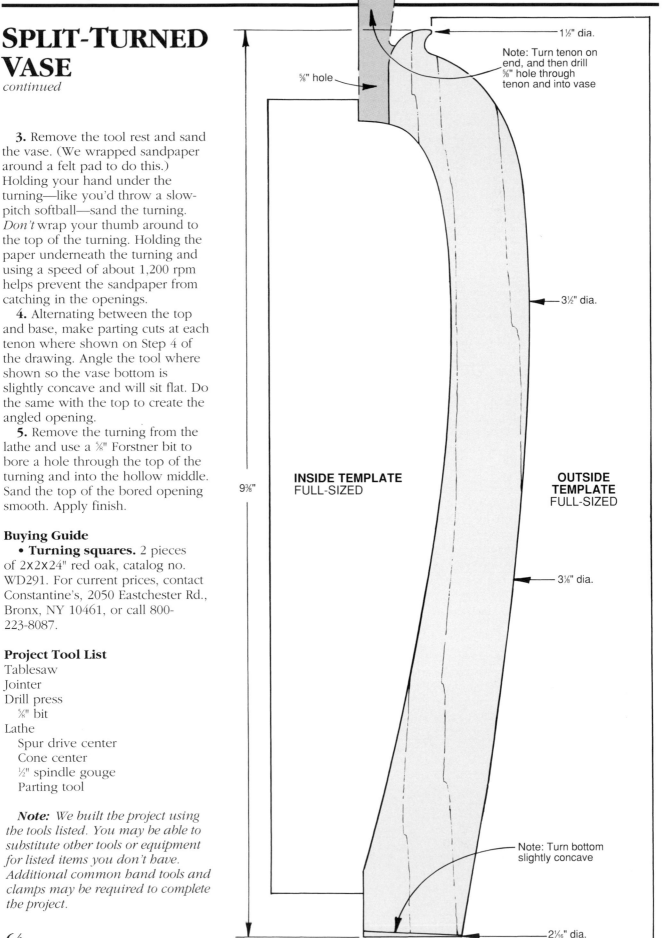

⅝" hole

1½" dia.

Note: Turn tenon on end, and then drill ⅝" hole through tenon and into vase

3½" dia.

9⅜"

INSIDE TEMPLATE
FULL-SIZED

OUTSIDE TEMPLATE
FULL-SIZED

3⅛" dia.

Note: Turn bottom slightly concave

2¹⁄₁₆" dia.

CANDLE HOLDERS WITH A FLARE

Armed with a degree in woodworking and furniture design from Indiana University of Pennsylvania, Mark Burhans headed for the lathe to put his knowledge and skills to work. Now, this full-time turner/furnituremaker markets a line of turned candle holders and weed vases. Mark, who lives in Athens, Ohio, prefers the local Appalachian hardwoods, such as cherry and walnut, for his creations.

Mount the stock and turn it to shape

Mark starts by fastening a 3×3×4½" block to his 3" faceplate. "I use a 1" spindle gouge ground to a 50° angle for roughing the block to a cylinder," Mark says. "All that's required is a

sharp edge, a light touch, and good eye protection." With a parting tool and a lathe speed of 1,200 rpm, Mark trues up the top (the end opposite the faceplate) of the holder. Then, he switches to a ½" spindle gouge to turn the exterior to shape. A skew is used to form the V-cut for the base. (Make a full-sized template for help if necessary.)

Mark then moves the tailstock around to the end of the candle holder and calls on a parting tool to form the tapered opening. Smooth cuts leave the Ohio turner with little sanding before parting the holder from the waste stock.

Flaring the tulip top comes next

Mark supports the neck of the candle holder with a ⅜"-thick piece of stock, and cuts a kerf ⅜" into the center of the holder where shown in the drawing *below left*. Moving to a 1×42" strip sander, he slips the belt into the kerf and sands at an angle to flare the opening. Although it would take a bit more elbow grease, you also could file the opening to shape.

"I smooth the sanded edges and finish-shape the flared top with a coarse and then a fine half-round file," says Mark (see the photo *above right*). "Next, I wipe on a coat of Danish oil and let it dry. Finally, I buff the candle holder with a muslin buffing wheel loaded with tripoli (a jeweler's polishing compound)."

Project Tool List
Bandsaw
Strip sander
Lathe
    Faceplate
    Roughing gouge
    ½" spindle gouge
    ¾" skew chisel
    Parting tool

Note: *We built the project using the tools listed. You may be able to*

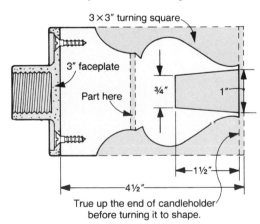

3 × 3" turning square

3" faceplate

Part here

¾"

1"

1½"

4½"

True up the end of candleholder before turning it to shape.

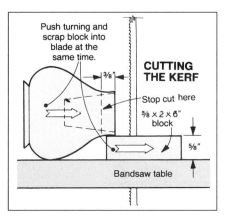

Push turning and scrap block into blade at the same time.

CUTTING THE KERF

⅜"

Stop cut here

⅜ × 2 × 6" block

⅝"

Bandsaw table

Mark employs half-round files to smooth the belt-sanded edges of each candle holder.

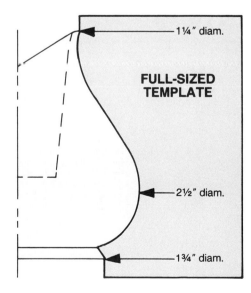

1¼" diam.

FULL-SIZED TEMPLATE

2½" diam.

1¾" diam.

substitute other tools or equipment for listed items you don't have. Additional common hand tools and clamps may be required to complete the project.

TURNED ROLLING PIN AND STORAGE RACK

Roll out pastries, cookies, or bread dough in high style with this hefty maple rolling pin adorned with easy-rotating walnut handles. As an added bonus, build our wall-mounted maple holder to display your lathe skills and keep the rolling pin within arm's reach.

Note: You'll need thick stock to make this project. You can either laminate thinner stock to the sizes listed in the Bill of Materials or use the Buying Guide on page 68. We've called the folks at Constantine's, and they've put together a rolling-pin kit for you.

Rough-shape the barrel

1. Cut a 3x3" maple turning square to 11½" long for the barrel (A).

2. Mark diagonals on each end of the barrel to locate centers. On *one* end, draw a 2¾"-diameter circle. Remove most of the stock *outside* the marked circle by bevel-ripping the edges using a table saw with its blade set at 45°. (Use the circle drawn on the end of the barrel as a guide when trimming the waste.)

3. Remove the spur center from the lathe headstock, and replace it with a chuck fitted with a ½" brad-point bit. Fit the tailstock with a cone center. Move the tailstock next to the barrel, and align the marked center point on the end of the barrel with the brad-point bit. Using a handscrew clamp, clamp the barrel level as shown *right*.

4. With the lathe set at its slowest speed, drill a 2½"-deep hole in the barrel. You'll need to turn the lathe off periodically, remove the shavings, and then resume drilling. (We wrapped tape on the bit to ensure drilling to an accurate depth.) Turn the barrel-clamp assembly around, and fit the hole just drilled onto the cone center. Check that the bit

aligns with the marked center point, and drill a second 2½"-deep hole. Set the barrel aside for now.

Make 2 turning centers

1. Cut two pieces of ¾" hardwood to ¾" square by 2¾" long for the turning centers (B). Mark diagonals on both ends of each piece to locate centers. On *one* end of each turning center, cut kerfs ⅛" deep along each marked diagonal with a hand saw. Punch a hole

Drill a ½" hole 2½" deep centered in each end of the maple barrel.

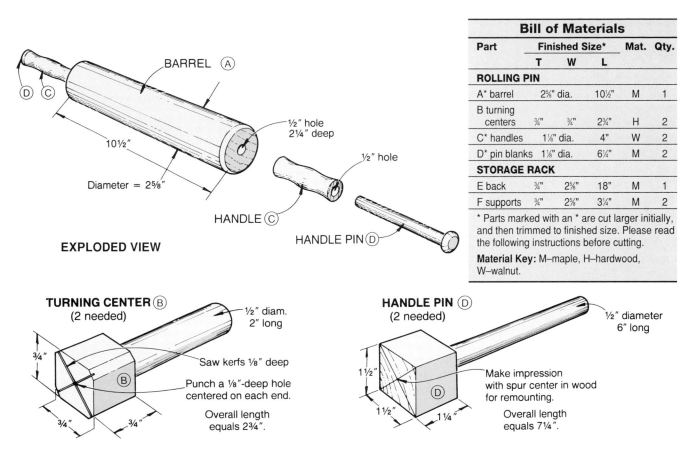

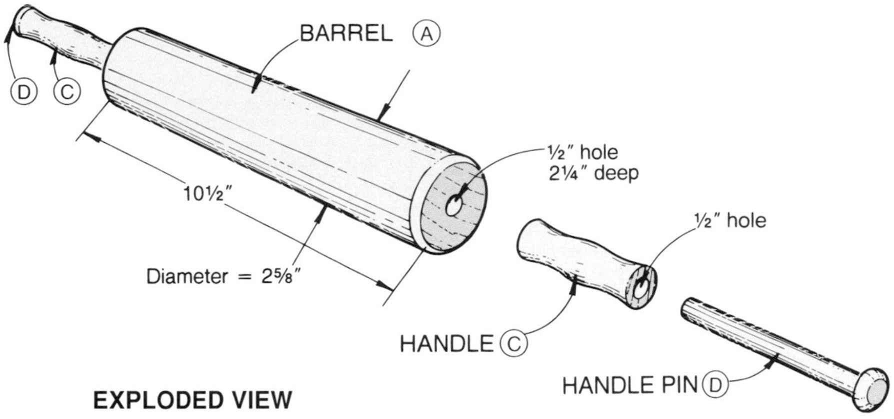
BARREL (A)
(D) (C)
10½″
Diameter = 2⅝″
½″ hole
2¼″ deep
½″ hole
HANDLE (C)
HANDLE PIN (D)

EXPLODED VIEW

Bill of Materials					
Part	Finished Size* T	W	L	Mat.	Qty.
ROLLING PIN					
A* barrel	2⅝" dia.		10½"	M	1
B turning centers	¾"	¾"	2¾"	H	2
C* handles	1⅛" dia.		4"	W	2
D* pin blanks	1⅛" dia.		6¼"	M	2
STORAGE RACK					
E back	¾"	2⅝"	18"	M	1
F supports	¾"	2⅝"	3¼"	M	2

* Parts marked with an * are cut larger initially, and then trimmed to finished size. Please read the following instructions before cutting.

Material Key: M–maple, H–hardwood, W–walnut.

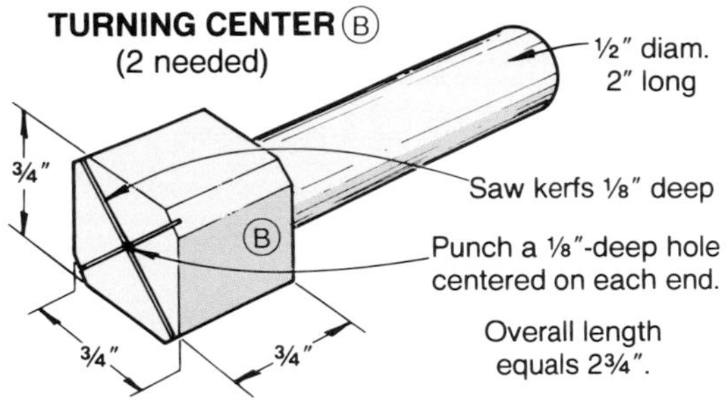
TURNING CENTER (B)
(2 needed)
½″ diam.
2″ long
¾″
Saw kerfs ⅛″ deep
Punch a ⅛″-deep hole
centered on each end.
¾″
¾″
Overall length
equals 2¾″.

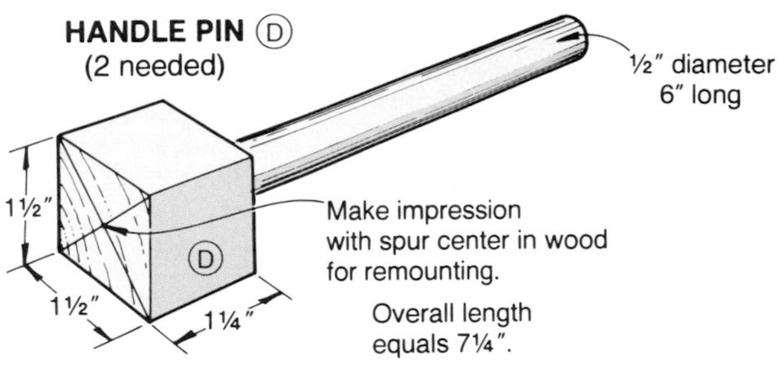
HANDLE PIN (D)
(2 needed)
½″ diameter
6″ long
1½″
Make impression
with spur center in wood
for remounting.
1½″
1¼″
Overall length
equals 7¼″.

about ⅛" deep in the center of each end of each turning center with an awl or center punch.

2. Mount one of the turning centers between centers on the lathe, and turn the stock to the shape and size shown on the Turning Center drawing. Now, sand the shank portion of the turning center to ½", checking the diameter often with an outside caliper to make sure you end up with a snug fit in the ½" hole in the barrel. Repeat for the second turning center.

Finish-turning the maple barrel

1. Push the turning centers into the holes in the barrel. Mount the assembly between centers. Start the lathe, and turn the barrel to a cylinder 2⅝" in diameter.

2. Trim each end of the barrel with a parting tool for a finished-barrel length of 10½". Be careful to stop the cut once the parting tool makes contact with the turning center.

3. Using a sanding block, sand the barrel to remove any waviness. Sand the ends smooth, sanding a slight round-over on the corners.

4. Apply a liberal coat of cooking oil to the barrel, and let the oil soak in for a few minutes. Wipe off any excess oil with a clean rag. Turn your lathe on, and polish the barrel to a high luster by holding a clean white rag against the wood. Repeat with a second coat of oil.

Shape the walnut handles and maple pins

1. Cut two pieces of 1½"-thick walnut to 1½" wide by 4⅛" long for the handles (C). Mark diagonals on each end of each handle to locate centers. Clamp one of the handle blanks in a handscrew clamp. Check that the handle blank is square with the drill press table. Then, center and drill a ½" hole through the length of each handle. (To keep the bit from wandering, we used a brad-point bit.)

2. Cut two pieces of 1½"-thick maple to 1½" wide by 7¼" long for the pin blanks (D).

3. Mount one of the pin blanks between centers, and mark a reference line 1¼" from the headstock end. Turn the pin to the shape shown *above*. Spot-glue one of the handle blanks onto a handle pin (we used hot-melt glue).

4. Mount the handle and pin assembly between centers using the marks on the drive center and pin to locate their original position. Turn the handle to the shape shown on the Handle drawing on *page 68*. True up the end of the handle nearest the tailstock. Sand the handle, and apply an oil finish.

5. Separate the handle from the pin by cutting the glue joint with your parting tool. Stop the cut as soon as you cut through the walnut.

6. Remove the handle from the pin and remount the handle pin between centers. Sand the handle-pin shaft so the handle will turn easily on the pin shaft. (We stopped the lathe several times to check the fit of the handle on the handle pin.) Shape the end of the handle pin where shown on the Exploded View and Handle drawings.

7. Place the handle on the pin, and remount them between centers. Sand the head of the pin to

continued

TURNED ROLLING PIN AND STORAGE RACK
continued

the same diameter as the end of the handle (see the Handle drawing). Finally, use your skew to cut the pin free. Sand the rounded end of the pin smooth.

Final assembly

1. Apply oil to the inside of the hole in each handle (C) and to the ends of the handle. Apply oil to all but the 2" of the pin (D) that will be glued into the barrel.

2. Spread a light coat of glue in the holes in the barrel (we used a cotton swab). Slip the handles on the pins, and carefully tap the pins in place, leaving just enough play for the handles to turn freely. Immediately back out slightly if too tight.

Building the maple storage rack

We were so impressed with the good looks of the rolling pin, we decided to add a wall-mounted storage rack. To make the maple rack, cut the back (E) and supports (F) to the sizes listed in the Bill of Materials. Mark the radii on the back piece, and cut it to shape. Now, mark the location, cut two dadoes, and drill the holes in the back where shown on the Storage Rack drawing *below*. Use carbon paper to transfer the full-sized pattern onto the two support pieces (F). Cut the supports to shape, sand smooth, and glue them into the dadoes. Finish-sand, apply the finish, and hang.

Buying Guide

• **Rolling pin kit.** 1½x1½x12" walnut, 3x3x12" maple, 1½x1½x18" maple. Kit no. WD988. For current prices, contact Constantine's, 2050 Eastchester Rd., Bronx, NY 10461, or call 800-223-8087.

Project Tool List
Tablesaw
Bandsaw or scrollsaw
Lathe
  Spur drive center
  Revolving tail center
  Drill chuck with ½" bit
  ⅜", ½", ¾", spindle gouges
  1" skew
  Parting tool

Note: We built the project using the tools listed. You may be able to substitute other tools or equipment for listed items you don't have. Additional common hand tools and clamps may be required to complete the project.

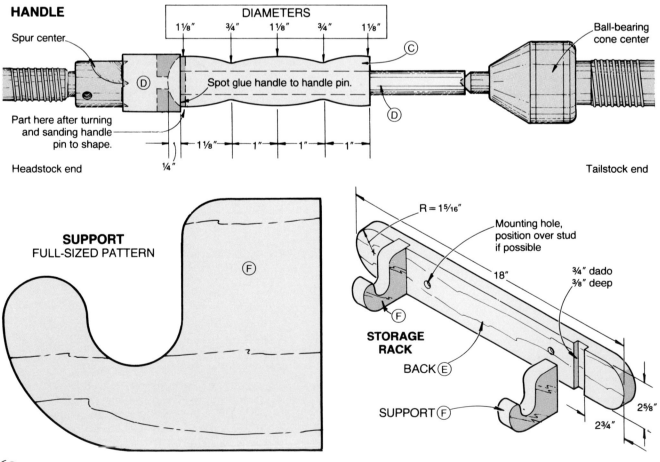

EXOTIC WOOD NAPKIN RINGS

Exotic hardwood from Latin America puts bread on the table for California lumber merchant Mitch Talcove. Mitch contracts for logs, harvested from Central America and Mexico, and cuts them in his sawmill in Puerto Vallarta, Mexico. In his spare time, Mitch thinks up creative ways to use valuable sawmill scraps.

First, shape a tapered, softwood mandrel

Cut a piece of softwood 1½" square by about 8" long for the mandrel. "A fir or pine 2×4 works well," Mitch notes. "A softwood will compress slightly and keep the napkin blank snugly attached when turning it to shape. Harder woods won't compress as well." Mark a center point on each end of the mandrel, and mount it between centers on the lathe. Turn the stock round with a ½" gouge, and taper the mandrel to the dimensions shown on the drawing.

Here's how to turn the rings

For ease in turning round, bevel-rip the edges of a 2×2×12" turning square (see the Buying Guide for our source) on the table saw. Cut the napkin ring blanks to 1¾" long. Find and mark the centerpoint on one end of each blank. Using a drill press and a Forstner bit, bore a 1¼" hole through the center of each napkin blank.

Remove the tapered mandrel from the lathe, and slide a napkin ring blank onto it until it fits snugly. Now, twist the blank clockwise to lock it in place. Turn the blank round with a ½" gouge and form the slight tapers on each ring with a skew. Mitch prefers a wall thickness of about ⅛".

To sand the inside of each napkin ring, Mitch makes his own sanding drums. Here's how to do it: Wrap double-faced tape around a ½"-diameter piece of dowel stock 3" long. Then, adhere 100-grit sandpaper to the tape, chuck the dowel into your drill press, and sand the inside of each napkin ring. Now, slide one napkin ring back onto the mandrel, start the lathe, and hand-sand the outside of it, progressing to 400-grit paper. Stop the lathe and do the final sanding with the grain. Repeat for the other rings.

Now, apply finish to the napkin rings. Mitch likes to finish his with Liberon Black Bison Clear Wax, although any high-content carnauba wax would work. Next, loosen the tailstock, and remove the mandrel from the lathe. Carefully twist the napkin ring counterclockwise to separate it from the holder. Then, apply wax to the inside of the ring.

Buying Guide

• **Turning square.** Five-piece special of 2×2×12" squares in choice of bocote, cocobolo, bubinga, lignum vitae, or purpleheart. For current prices, contact Tropical Exotic Hardwoods of Latin America, P.O. Box 1806, Carlsbad, CA 92008, or call 619-434-3030.

Project Tool List:

Drill press
  1¼" bit
Lathe
  Spur drive center
  Rotating tail center
  ½" spindle gouge
  ½" skew chisel

Note: We built the project using the tools listed. You may be able to substitute other tools or equipment for listed items you don't have. Additional common hand tools and clamps may be required to complete the project.

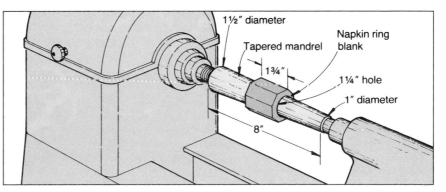

TURN A BERNSON SHOWCASE VASE

Bruce Bernson, a self-taught woodturner, lives near the beautiful coastal city of Santa Barbara, California. He has been known to search as far as Oregon for uniquely grained woods such as wild lilac and buckeye burl for his turnings. He's even found some turning "treasures" in such unlikely spots as land-clearing sites and along the seacoast after storms.

Bruce turned the vase shown *above* from a big-leaf maple burl dried in his own kiln (built from a 2,000-gallon gas tank).

Here's how Bruce turns this vase: "I start with a cube of wood approximately 4½" square. I band-saw the block to a cylindrical shape and mount the block between centers. Next, I turn it round, and remove stock from the ends to form two dowel-like supports."

Bruce uses a ½" roundnose scraper to form the sweeping neck and bulbous body. (See the Full-sized Half pattern *below right,* and the drawing *below.*)

To finish the vase, this craftsman turns it as smooth as possible on the lathe, and hand-sands it, using as fine as 600-grit paper. He then removes the turning from the lathe, cuts off the dowel-like projections, and drills a ⁹⁄₁₆" hole 3" deep for a test tube in the center of the top.

As Bruce explains, "I apply a single coat of Watco Danish Oil to the vase and allow it to dry for three days." Still not satisfied, Bruce then applies tripoli to a 10"-diameter cotton pad mounted to an arbor, and hand-holds the vase against the spinning pad to buff it. At a point where most people would call it quits, Bruce proceeds to use a lamb's-wool bonnet mounted to another arbor, where he applies a coat of pure carnuba wax to the burl vase.

"Finally," Bruce concludes, "I use white glue to adhere a piece of protective leather to the bottom of the vase. After the glue has dried, I trim away the excess leather with a sharp utility razor blade. I then sign and number the vase in the wood along the leather base with a woodburning tool."

Dried flowers can be displayed in the weed pot as it is. Or, for flower buds, insert a ½×3" test tube into the hole.

Project Tool List:
Bandsaw
Drill press
  ⁹⁄₁₆" bit
Lathe
  Spur drive center
  Rotating tail center
  ½" spindle gouge
  ½" roundnose scraper
  Parting tool

Note: *We built the project using the tools listed. You may be able to substitute other tools or equipment for listed items you don't have. Additional common hand tools and clamps may be required to complete the project.*

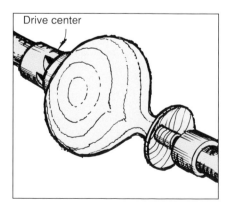

Drive center

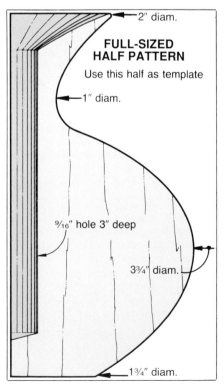

2" diam.

FULL-SIZED HALF PATTERN

Use this half as template

1" diam.

⁹⁄₁₆" hole 3" deep

3¾" diam.

1¾" diam.

TURNED MORTAR AND PESTLE

For thousands of years, cooks have ground herbs, seeds, and spices in utensils like the one below, and then sprinkled the tasty morsels on their creations. Our mortar and pestle lets you continue the tradition, accenting your kitchen's decor and your meals.

Start with the pestle

1. Using carbon paper or a photocopy and spray-on adhesive, transfer the full-sized Pestle and Mortar Template patterns on *page 73* to thin cardboard. Using a crafts knife (we used an X-acto knife), carefully cut the templates to shape. Set the templates aside for now.

2. Square one end, and then crosscut a 7½" length from a 2" turning square. (We used maple.) Draw diagonal lines on each end of the turning square to find the center. Mount the piece between centers on your lathe, and then turn it round (we used a ½" gouge and a lathe speed of about 1,000 rpm).

3. Next, increase the lathe speed to about 1,200 to 1,500 rpm. Now, as shown at *right,* turn the pestle to shape using a ⅜" gouge, and the pestle template for reference. Sand the pestle smooth. (We used 100-, 150-, and 220-grit sandpaper.)

4. Wipe off the dust, and apply a coat of water-resistant finish to the pestle. (We used Behlen's Salad Bowl Finish [see the Buying Guide for a source] and applied it by hand with a piece of clean, used nylon hose.) Let the finish dry (overnight), and then using fine steel wool or 600-grit sandpaper, lightly sand the finish. Apply a second and third coat, and again, lightly sand, wiping off the dust between coats.

5. To separate the pestle, make a parting cut at the bottom end to separate the turning from the bottom waste where shown on the Pestle Blank drawing on *page 72.* Using a fine-toothed saw or

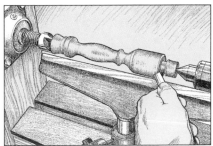

bandsaw, cut the top end of the pestle. Now, hand-sand the top and bottom ends of the pestle smooth and apply finish to the bare ends.

Next, turn the mortar to shape

1. Make a 3"-diameter auxiliary wooden faceplate and fit it to your lathe's 3" faceplate. (We made ours by bandsawing a 3"-diameter disc out of a ¾"-thick piece of solid wood scrap, and then screwing it to the faceplate.)

2. To save turning work, round off the corners on a 4"-square, 4"-thick bowl blank. (We used our jointer and disc sander to cut down the four sharp corners.) Center and glue (we used 5-minute epoxy) one end of the bowl blank (we used

ash for its decorative grain but suggest using a more commonly available wood if you can not buy ash locally; see the Buying Guide for a source of native-wood blanks) onto the auxiliary faceplate as shown on the Mortar Blank Drawing on *page 72.* If you can't buy turning stock locally, or don't want to order it by mail, you can make your own blank. Simply cut five pieces of ¾"-thick stock to 4¼" square. Apply glue to the mating faces, align the edges, and then clamp the pieces.

3. Thread the faceplate assembly onto your lathe's headstock. Slide the tailstock against the mortar blank, and lock it in position. The tailstock offers extra stability while turning the mortar exterior.

4. Finish-turn the mortar blank round. (We used a ¾" roughing gouge and a speed of about 700 rpm. Then, we switched to a ½" gouge and turned the blank to 3¾" diameter, checking the diameter as we turned with an outside caliper.)

continued

TURNED MORTAR AND PESTLE
continued

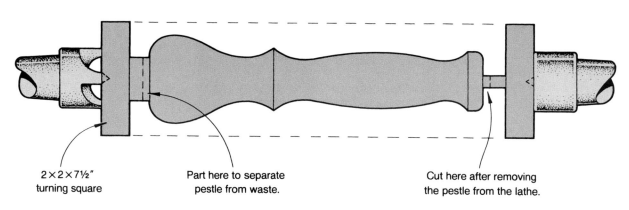

2×2×7½″
turning square

Part here to separate
pestle from waste.

Cut here after removing
the pestle from the lathe.

PESTLE BLANK

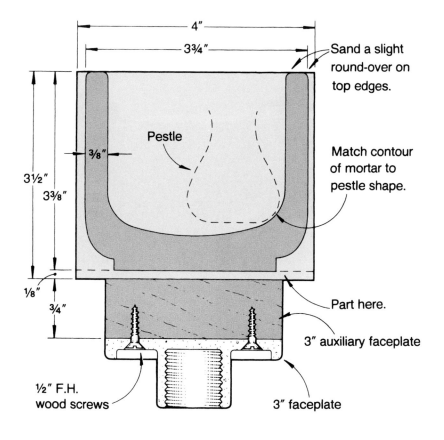

4″

3¾″

Sand a slight
round-over on
top edges.

Pestle

Match contour
of mortar to
pestle shape.

3⅜″

3½″

3⅜″

⅛″

¾″

Part here.

3″ auxiliary faceplate

½″ F.H.
wood screws

3″ faceplate

MORTAR BLANK

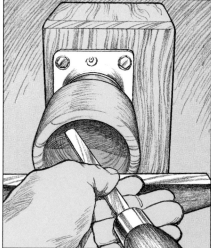

5. Using a parting tool, form the recessed base, comparing the shape with the mortar template. Increase the lathe speed to about 1,500 rpm, and sand the mortar's exterior. (We sanded the mortar with the lathe running, then stopped it, and used a palm sander as shown *above right,* to finish-sand the end grain.)

6. Stop the lathe, back the tailstock away, adjust lathe speed to about 1,000 rpm, and position the tool rest at the end of the mor-tar blank. Next, using a ⅜″ bowl gouge, turn the mortar cavity to shape as shown *above.* Keep the wall straight and a uniform ⅜″ thick as dimensioned on the Mortar Blank drawing. Shape the bottom inside curve of the mortar to match the curvature of the pestle bottom (see the Mortar Blank drawing *opposite*).

7. Increase lathe speed to 1,500 rpm, and sand the inside of the mortar smooth. Sand a round-over on the top edges of the mortar where shown on the Mortar Blank drawing.

8. Apply the finish to the mortar, using the same process used to finish the pestle. For best results when crushing seeds and spices, use fine steel wool and slightly rough up the finish on the bottom of the mortar. Don't rub through the finish. Just remove the sheen to make a less slippery surface.

9. Adjust the lathe's speed to about 800 rpm, and then carefully part the mortar from the faceplate, catching the piece in your right hand as it comes free. Sand the mortar bottom smooth, and apply finish to the bottom surface.

Note: You'll need to apply a new coat or two of the finish when you notice it wearing thin. To apply a new coat, lightly sand or rub the entire surface with steel wool. Apply the finish and let dry overnight. Add a second coat of finish if necessary.

Buying Guide
• **Turning stock.** One 4"-square by 4"-thick bowl blank and one 2x2x8" turning square. Available in walnut, cherry, and maple. For current prices, contact Constantine's, 2050 Eastchester Rd. Bronx, NY 10461, or call 800-223-8087.

MORTAR TEMPLATE
Full-sized template

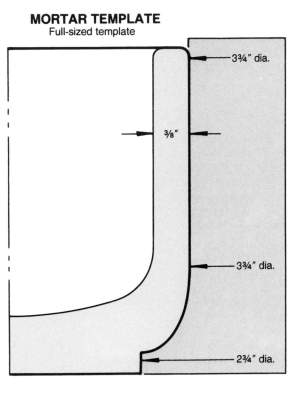

• **Behlen's Salad Bowl Finish.** FDA-approved, nontoxic finish for kitchen woodenware. One-pint container. Stock No. 85006. For current price, contact Armor Products, Box 445, East Northport, NY 11731, or call 516-462-6228.

Project Tool List
Lathe
  Spur drive center
  Revolving tail center
  Faceplate
  ¾" roughing gouge
  ⅜", ½" spindle gouges
  ⅜" bowl gouge
  Parting tool
Finishing sander

Note: We built the project using the tools listed. You may be able to substitute other tools or equipment for listed items you don't have. Additional common hand tools and clamps may be required to complete the project.

PESTLE TEMPLATE
Full-sized template

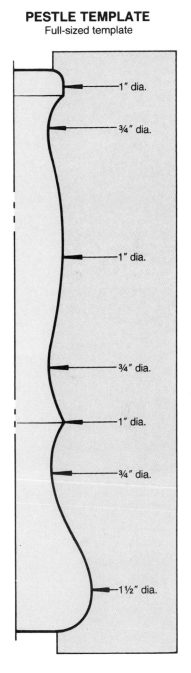

LATHE-LAID EGGS

Now, you're ready to form the lid and base

1. Remove the cylinder from between centers, fit one tenoned end into your homemade chuck, and tighten the hose clamp to secure it. Move the tailstock into position, centered on the opposite end. Now, use a parting tool to cut the workpiece in two where shown in Figure B. Set aside the half closest to the tailstock; you'll use this later for the base. Back the tailstock away from the workpiece.

2. Hollow the lid to the shape shown in Figure C. (We used a ⅜" gouge and a round-nosed scraper.) For a tight fit against the base later, turn the first ³⁄₁₆" of the interior flat where shown on the Interior detail. Sand smooth, being careful not to round the flat area. Add the finish to the lid interior.

Be prepared to hear, "How did you do that?" when you show off this nifty hollow-egg container. Our secret (and now it's yours) lies in the use of the handy, homemade lathe chuck featured on *pages 6–7*.

OK, let's get going

1. Start with a 2½"-square block of hardwood 5" long. If you don't have a kiln-dried turning square this size, laminate thinner stock.

2. Draw diagonals from corner to corner on each end, and mount the block between centers on your lathe. At a speed of about 800 rpm, use a gouge or skew to turn the block to a diameter of 2".

3. As shown in Figure A, turn a ½"-long tenon on each end to a diameter that will fit *snugly* into your homemade chuck. Our tenons measured 1½" in diameter; yours may differ slightly. (We used an outside calipers to measure the diameter, and frequently removed the block to test-fit the tenons in the chuck.)

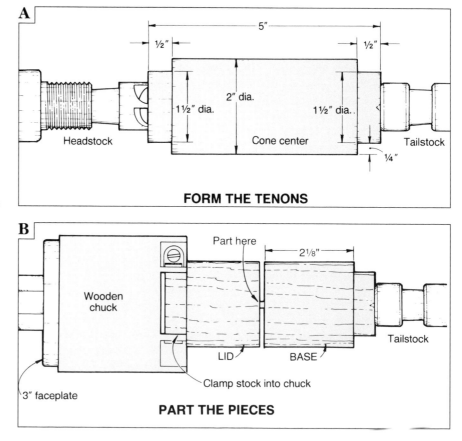

A

5"

½"   ½"

1½" dia.   2" dia.   1½" dia.

¼"

Headstock   Cone center   Tailstock

FORM THE TENONS

B

Part here

2⅛"

Wooden chuck

LID   BASE

Clamp stock into chuck

3" faceplate   Tailstock

PART THE PIECES

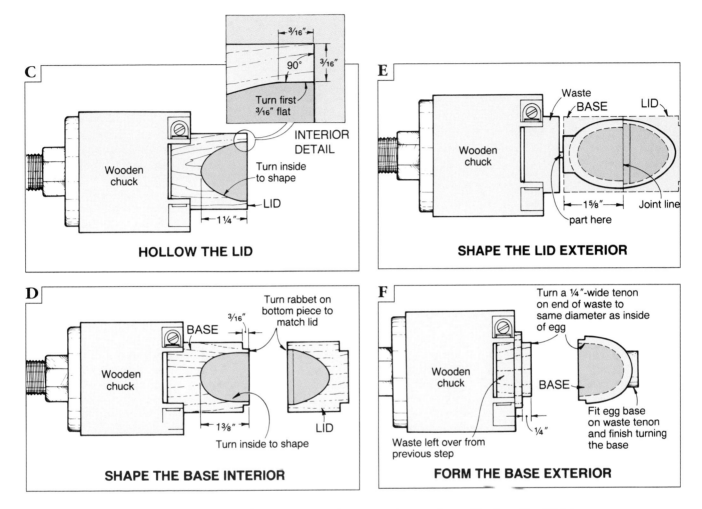

C

⅜6″

90°

³⁄₁₆″

Turn first ³⁄₁₆″ flat

INTERIOR DETAIL

Turn inside to shape

Wooden chuck

LID

1¼″

HOLLOW THE LID

E

Waste

BASE

LID

Wooden chuck

1⅝″

part here

Joint line

SHAPE THE LID EXTERIOR

D

³⁄₁₆″

BASE

Turn rabbet on bottom piece to match lid

Wooden chuck

LID

1⅜″

Turn inside to shape

SHAPE THE BASE INTERIOR

F

Turn a ¼″-wide tenon on end of waste to same diameter as inside of egg

Wooden chuck

BASE

¼″

Waste left over from previous step

Fit egg base on waste tenon and finish turning the base

FORM THE BASE EXTERIOR

3. Fit the base tenon into the chuck, and use a parting tool or a square-end scraper to form a ³⁄₁₆″ rabbet that will fit snugly into the lid interior where shown in Figure D. Make light cuts to avoid removing too much material and making the rabbet too small, which would result in a sloppy fit. (We stopped frequently to test-fit the lid on the base.) Then, hollow the base interior to the shape shown in Figure D.

4. Fit the lid firmly onto the base where shown in Figure E. Turn the lid exterior to shape, sand smooth on the lathe, and add the finish. Pull the lid from the base and set it aside.

5. Shape a portion of the base exterior to the shape shown in Figure E. Part the base from the chuck where shown.

6. On the waste piece left in the chuck, turn a tenon to fit snugly inside the base piece where shown in Figure F. Fit the base onto the waste piece and finish turning the base to shape. Sand smooth and add the finish.

Project Tool List

Lathe
   Spur drive center
   Revolving tail center
   Wooden chuck (See *pages 6–7*)
   ⅜″, ½″ spindle gouges
   ½″ roundnose scraper
   Parting tool

Note: We built the project using the tools listed. You may be able to substitute other tools or equipment for listed items you don't have. Additional common hand tools and clamps may be required to complete the project.

SPIRITED FOURSOME OF YULETIDE TURNINGS

Let's build a snowman

1. Locate and mark the centerpoint on each end of a 1½" turning square about 3½" long. Mount the square between your lathe centers, and then turn it to a 1¼" cylinder with the ½" gouge.

2. Using the template, mark sections for the three beads and the top hat, and then turn them to shape with the spear-point tool or a gouge. Finish-cut with the ¼" skew. Cut in to ⅛" at the top and bottom with the parting tool.

3. Next, sand the snowman with 150-, 220-, and then 320-grit sandpaper. Remove your turning from the lathe, saw off the waste, and sand the ends flat.

As the tree turns

1. Start the tree with a 1½" square about 4" long. Turn it to 1⅜" diameter, and then, using your template, mark off the 2½" body section and the ¾" trunk.

2. Taper the body section to about ¼" at the top. Now, shape the tree by cutting a series of partial cones with the ¼" skew chisel.

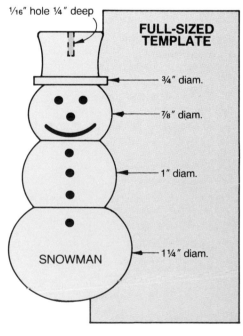

1/16" hole ¼" deep

FULL-SIZED TEMPLATE

¾" diam.

⅞" diam.

1" diam.

SNOWMAN

1¼" diam.

Turner Ron Odegaard has been making tree ornaments from small bits of hardwood for more than 15 years. "If I make a piece of furniture, I often have enough scraps left over to make ornaments," Ron said. He also gathers scraps from other woodworkers near his Appleton, Wisconsin, home rather than see potential turnings buried in a landfill or burned. Here are four of Ron's favorite ornaments.

To start, copy the full-sized templates, at *right* and *opposite,* to posterboard, and then cut them out with an X-acto knife. You can adapt the designs to fit larger or smaller pieces of wood, too.

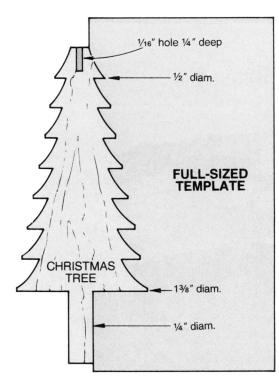

1/16" hole 1/4" deep

1/2" diam.

**FULL-SIZED
TEMPLATE**

**CHRISTMAS
TREE**

1 3/8" diam.

1/4" diam.

Starting at the bottom of the body, space cuts a skew width apart. Turn the trunk to 1/4" diameter.

3. Sand with progressively finer grits, but be careful—the sharp edges of your turning can cut just like rotary knives. Part in to about 1/8" at top and bottom, remove the tree from the lathe, cut off the waste, and sand the ends

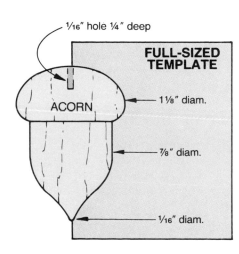

1/16" hole 1/4" deep

**FULL-SIZED
TEMPLATE**

ACORN

1 1/8" diam.

7/8" diam.

1/16" diam.

An acorn from two woods

1. Glue together two 1½ x 1½ x 1" pieces of contrasting woods to make 1½ x 1½ x 2" stock for the acorn. Turn the blank between centers to 1⅛" diameter. Shape the acorn with the ¼" skew, placing the division between top and bottom right at the glued joint. Sand and remove the turning.

Make a holiday chime

1. Begin the bell with a 2 x 2 x 3" square, and then round it to 1¾" diameter. Mark off a 2" section for the bell, and then turn a tenon on the waste end to fit your chuck. (If you don't have a lathe chuck, square the waste end and mount the turning on a screw point.)

2. Turn the bell to shape with a gouge, checking with your template. Then, hollow it out with the ½" round-point chisel. Cut the grooves with the ¼" skew.

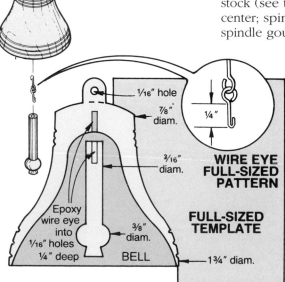

1/16" hole

7/8" diam.

3/16" diam.

1/4"

**WIRE EYE
FULL-SIZED
PATTERN**

Epoxy wire eye into 1/16" holes 1/4" deep

3/8" diam.

**FULL-SIZED
TEMPLATE**

BELL

1 3/4" diam.

3. To burn in the grooves, firmly tie each end of a piece of wire—single-strand picture-hanging wire about 12" long works well—to a length of dowel. With the lathe running, stretch the wire and press it into each groove.

4. Sand and remove from the lathe. File or sand flat sides on the hanging tab, 1/8" thick. Turn the clapper from 3/8"-diameter stock.

Finish them all up

1. Bend five wire eyes (see pattern, *below*) for each set of four ornaments. Link two to hinge the bell clapper. Drill 1/16" holes where shown on the patterns with a brad-point bit in a drill press.

2. Coat the shank of the wire eye with epoxy before inserting it into the ornament. Assemble the bell and clapper with the linked eyes, gluing each into place.

3. Put thick paint on with a toothpick for the snowman's face and buttons. Apply a clear finish to your ornaments, and then hang them on the front of your tree for all to see.

Supplies

Various small pieces of turning stock (see text). Chuck or screw center; spindle centers; 3/8" or 1/2" spindle gouge; 1/4" skew; 1/2" spear point; 1/2" round point; 1/4" parting tool; 1/16" drill bit; picture-hanging wire; calipers; ruler.

Lathe speeds

Roughing, 800–1,000 rpm; finishing and sanding, 1,250–1,700 rpm.

A BEVY
OF BOWLS

Here is a selection of bowl projects that features designs to suit a variety of tastes and purposes. Decorative—and useful too—this section will help you produce bowls that will become a point of pride in any household.

SOUTHWEST-INSPIRED BOWL

You won't make this bowl in an evening, in fact, it took us almost 30 hours to cut the pieces to size, glue them together, and then turn the bowl. But, you'd be hard-pressed to find a bowl of this quality for under $400.

Note: *Stack-laminated bowls require more planning than most turnings, but the spectacular results make them worth the effort. It's essential to read the stack-lamination techniques beginning on* page 50 *for in-depth information on the cutting, clamping, and turning processes needed to produce these stunning bowls. To avoid duplication, we frequently refer to photos in the techniques article.*

You'll need some thin stock for this project. You can plane or resaw thicker stock to the thicknesses stated in the Bill of Materials.

Cut and glue the parts for layers 1 through 6

1. Cut parts A–F to the sizes listed in the Bill of Materials. (Cut three of the seven Bs to length plus ¼".)

2. Position edge to edge the three Bs cut ¼" extra in length. Now, cut two pieces of plywood to 11½x4" to form the plywood clamping boards used to hold these three pieces flush while clamping. (As noted in the techniques article, if you don't use a coated-surface particleboard for the clamping boards, place waxed paper between the plywood and the pieces being clamped.) It is important that the pieces being laminated don't stick to the clamping boards.

3. Spread glue on the mating edges of the three pieces. Then, clamp the pieces edge to edge between the two pieces of plywood. (Refer to Photos A, B, and C in the techniques article for help with this and the following step.)

4. Remove the clamps, and trim both ends of the three-piece lamination to 4" in length (remember, measure length *with* the grain; the three-piece lamination should measure 4" long by 12" wide.)

5. To form layer 1, glue the three-piece lamination between two A pieces where shown on the Bowl Lamination drawing. Later, sand layer 1 flat as shown in Photo D on *page 52.*

6. To form layers 2 and 3, glue, clamp, and sand the pieces as just described. Note the grain direction shown on the Bowl Lamination drawing when cutting and clamping. Use the same procedure to form layers 4, 5, and 6.

7. As described and shown in Photo E on *page 52,* and dimensioned on the Bowl Lamination drawing, use a compass to mark a circle on the inside of each layer except for the bottom layer. Cut the circles to shape with a scrollsaw or portable jigsaw. Cutting the inside of the layers round reduces the amount of stock you'll need to remove when turning the inside of the bowl.

Now, tackle the feature layer

1. Fit a miter gauge with an auxiliary fence, and tilt your tablesaw blade 45° from vertical. Cut parts G through M from ¼"-thick stock to the sizes listed in the Bill of Materials. Glue and clamp each of the six individual layers together as shown in the photo on *page 80.*

2. Let each lamination dry for about an hour. Then, remove the

continued

CUTTING DIAGRAM

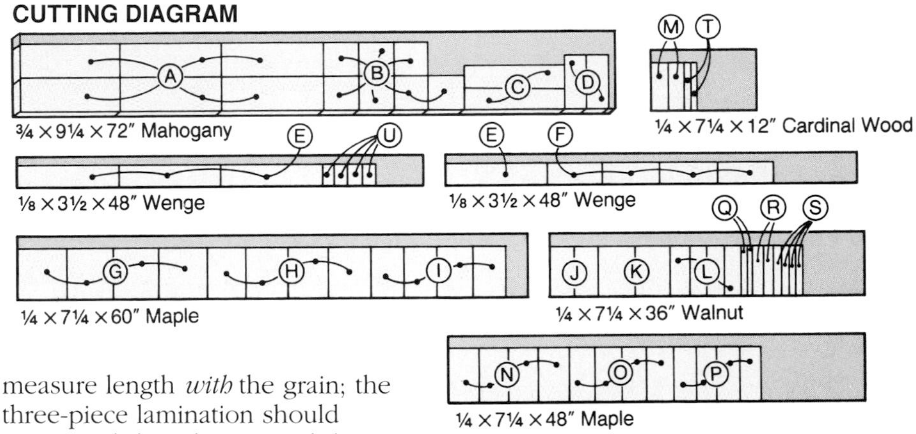

¾ × 9¼ × 72" Mahogany
¼ × 7¼ × 12" Cardinal Wood
⅛ × 3½ × 48" Wenge
⅛ × 3½ × 48" Wenge
¼ × 7¼ × 60" Maple
¼ × 7¼ × 36" Walnut
¼ × 7¼ × 48" Maple

Bill of Materials

Part	Initial size of pieces T	W	L	Mat.	Qty.
LAYERS 1 THROUGH 6					
A	¾"	4"	12"	MH	6
B	¾"	4"	4"	MH	7
C	¾"	2¾"	12"	MH	2
D	¾"	6½"	2¾"	MH	2
E	⅛"	2¾"	12"	WE	4
F	⅛"	2¾"	6½"	WE	4
SERRATED PATTERN					
G	¼"	6"	5⅜"	M	4
H	¼"	6"	4¾"	M	4
I	¼"	6"	3⅞"	M	4
J	¼"	6"	2¾"	W	2
K	¼"	0"	4"	W	2
L	¼"	6"	2¼"	W	4
M	¼"	6"	1¾"	CW	2
BLOCK PATTERN					
N	¼"	6"	3⅜"	M	4
O	¼"	6"	3"	M	4
P	¼"	6"	2⅝"	M	4
Q	¼"	6"	½"	W	2
R	¼"	6"	1¼"	W	2
S	¼"	6"	¾"	W	4
T	¼"	6"	½"	CW	2
U	⅛"	2$^{15}/_{16}$"	1½"	WE	4

Material Key: MH–mahogany, WE–wenge, M–maple, W–walnut, CW–cardinal wood

Supplies: coated plywood for clamping boards, plywood for auxiliary faceplate, ¼"-diameter dowel stock for guide pins, lacquer sanding sealer, polymerized tung oil, paste wax.

SOUTHWEST-INSPIRED BOWL

continued

Sandwich the parts being glued and clamped between two pieces of particleboard to keep them flat.

clamps and lightly sand each layer with 100-grit paper. Be careful not to sand depressions at the glue joints or to round-over the edges or ends of the layers when sanding. (To keep the layers flat, we found that a half-sheet finish sander works better than a palm sander.)

3. Mark a centerline on the top face of each layer, and transfer the line to both front and back edges. Align the centerlines and clamp the layers in the arrangement shown on the Serrated Pattern Lamination drawing. Check that the pattern aligns on both edges.

4. Measure 6" in both directions from the centerline and use a square to mark a line across each end of the stack. Using 3"-wide blocks for support, drill a ¼" guidepin hole on the outside of each marked line as shown in the photo on *page 82*. Remove the clamps, and cut two ¼"-diameter dowels to 2" long.

5. Spread an even coat of glue on the mating faces of the six layers. Insert the 2" dowels into the ¼" holes to realign the pieces, and clamp together the six layers.

6. Remove the clamps, and trim each end of the lamination where marked in Step 1 on the Serrated Pattern Lamination drawing. Using Step 2 on the same drawing for reference, rip the block in half.

Next, make the block-pattern lamination

1. Using a thin push block (ours measured less than ½" thick) as shown in the photo *opposite*,

cut to size parts N through T for the block-pattern lamination. Laminate each layer and then glue and clamp the individual layers to form the block, using the same process just described in Steps 1 through 6.

2. Cut four wenge parts (U) to the size listed in the Bill of Materials.

3. Glue and clamp the block-pattern laminations between serrated-pattern laminations with the wenge pieces in place where shown on the drawing on *page 82*. (We placed the pieces between two clamping boards to keep the faces of all the pieces flush.)

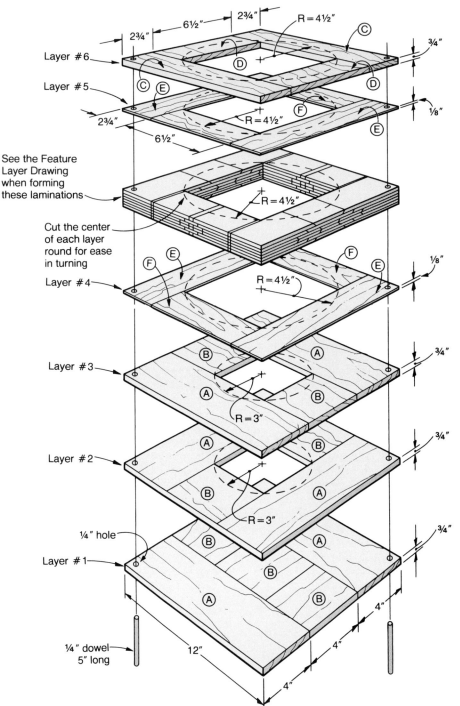

Layer #6

Layer #5

2¾"   6½"   2¾"

R = 4½"

Ⓒ Ⓓ

¾"

⅛"

2¾"   6½"

R = 4½"

Ⓒ Ⓔ   Ⓕ   Ⓔ

See the Feature Layer Drawing when forming these laminations

Cut the center of each layer round for ease in turning

R = 4½"

Layer #4

Ⓕ Ⓔ   R = 4½"   Ⓕ Ⓔ

⅛"

Layer #3

Ⓑ Ⓐ

Ⓐ Ⓑ

R = 3"

¾"

Layer #2

Ⓐ Ⓑ

Ⓑ Ⓐ

R = 3"

¾"

¼" hole

Layer #1

Ⓑ Ⓐ

Ⓐ Ⓑ

¾"

Ⓐ Ⓑ

¼" dowel 5" long

12"

4"

4"

4"

SERRATED PATTERN LAMINATION

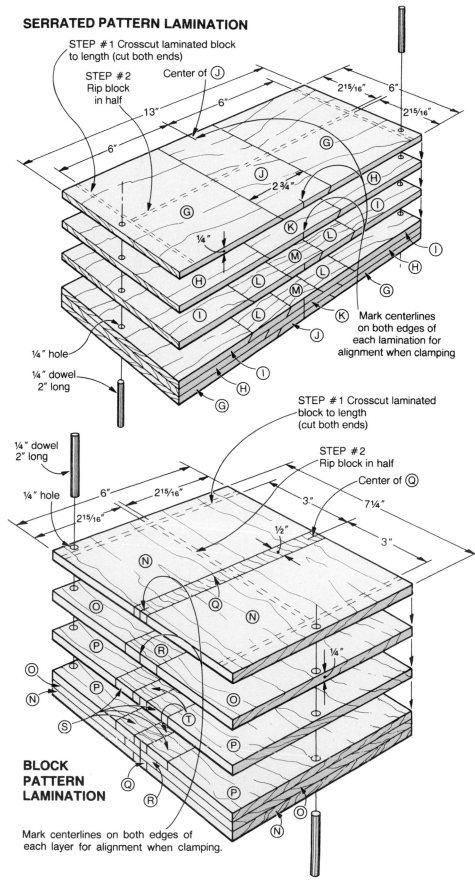

STEP #1 Crosscut laminated block to length (cut both ends)

STEP #2 Rip block in half

Center of (J)

13"

6"

6"

2¹⁵/₁₆"

6"

2¹⁵/₁₆"

Center of (J)

2¾"

¼"

G

J

G

H

I

K

L

M

L

M

L

L

H

I

K

J

I

H

G

¼" hole

¼" dowel 2" long

Mark centerlines on both edges of each lamination for alignment when clamping

¼" dowel 2" long

¼" hole

STEP #1 Crosscut laminated block to length (cut both ends)

STEP #2 Rip block in half

Center of (Q)

6"

2¹⁵/₁₆"

3"

7¼"

2¹⁵/₁₆"

½"

3"

¼"

N

Q

N

O

P

R

O

N

P

¼"

O

S

T

P

BLOCK PATTERN LAMINATION

Q

R

P

O

N

Mark centerlines on both edges of each layer for alignment when clamping.

For safety, use a thin push block when cutting to length the narrow block-pattern pieces.

4. Remove the clamps and sand the top and bottom faces of the feature lamination smooth and flush.

Here's how to form the bowl blank

1. Align the individual layers in the order shown on the Bowl Lamination drawing. Once in position, dry-clamp the layers.

2. As you did earlier with the feature layers, drill a pair of guide-pin holes through the dry-clamped assembly where shown on the Bowl Lamination drawing. Remove the clamps. Next, cut two pieces of ¼" dowel to 5" in length.

3. Spread an even coat of glue on all mating surfaces. Then, clamp the layers together, using the dowel guide pins to realign the pieces. See Photo H on *page 54* for help.

Turn the laminated-bowl blank to shape

1. With a compass, mark a 6" radius centered on the bottom of the bowl blank. Next, mark a 6¼" radius on a piece of ¾" plywood (we prefer Baltic birch) for the auxiliary faceplate. Bandsaw the bowl blank and auxiliary faceplate to shape.

2. Fasten the auxiliary faceplate to your 6" metal faceplate. Turn the auxiliary faceplate to a 6" diameter. Center and glue the bowl blank to the auxiliary faceplate. Let the project stand for 24 hours.

3. Using the Bowl Shape drawing on *page 82* as a guide, make a full-sized template on heavy paper or thin cardboard.

4. With your lathe running at about 500 rpm, shape the outside

continued

SOUTHWEST-INSPIRED BOWL
continued

FEATURE LAYER

2¹⁵/₁₆"
⅛"
12"
2¹⁵/₁₆"
R = 4½"
1½"
6"
1½"
2¹⁵/₁₆"
Block-patterned laminations
1½"
2¹⁵/₁₆"

Serrated-pattern laminations

Project Tool List
Tablesaw
Bandsaw
Scrollsaw or jigsaw
Drill press
 ¼" bit
Portable drill
 Sanding disc
 Finishing sander
 Lathe
  Faceplate
  Bowl gouge
  Side scraper
  Skew scraper
  Parting tool

Note: *We built the project using the tools listed. You may be able to substitute other tools or equipment for listed items you don't have. Additional common hand tools and clamps may be required to complete the project.*

After marking reference lines 6" from the marked centerline, drill two guide-pin holes in the patterned pieces to assure precise alignment when gluing.

of the bowl, frequently checking the shape of the bowl against the template. (We used a 1⅜" bullnosed scraper.) Then, shape the inside of the bowl. (We turned the bowl wall to a ½" thickness and then sanded the wall to ⅜" thick. Finally, we power-sanded the bowl as shown in Photo J on *page 55*.)

5. Finish the bowl. (We applied two coats of lacquer sanding sealer followed by several coats of polymerized tung oil.)

6. Now you're ready to part the bowl from the auxiliary faceplate by splitting the plywood one or two plies away from the bowl. We sug-

gest you ask a helper to steady the bowl while you carefully tap a 1" chisel with a mallet. Don't try to split a ply in the auxiliary faceplate by driving the chisel at just one point. Rather, tap the chisel, rotate the bowl and tap again. Repeat this operation at about four different locations around the faceplate until it splits easily.

7. Sand the bottom of the bowl smooth. Finish the bottom.

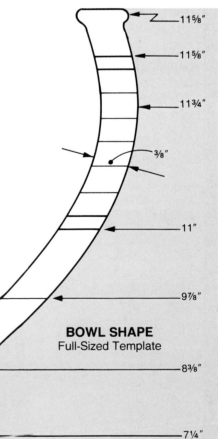

11⅝"
11⅝"
11¾"
⅜"
11"
9⅞"
BOWL SHAPE
Full-Sized Template
8⅜"
⅜"
7¼"

PEWTER-TOPPED POTPOURRI BOWL

Here's a project that makes scents. Turn this stylish bowl and fill it with potpourri—a fragrant mixture of flowers, herbs, and spices. Then, top it off with a rich-looking pewter lid. It's a project that not only looks great, it freshens the air, too.

1. Attach an auxiliary faceplate of ¾"-thick scrapwood to a 3" faceplate. Draw diagonal lines to locate the center on the back of a 3x6x6" bowl blank. Then, scribe a 3"-diameter circle (or one the size of your faceplate) and a 6"-diameter circle around the center. Bandsaw around the larger circle. Then, glue the faceplate to the workpiece inside the smaller circle, and mount it on your lathe.

2. Transfer the template *below right* to cardboard, and cut it out. With your ⅜" gouge, turn the blank to 5¼" diameter, and then to the profile. Square the edges of the raised band. To form the grooves, lay the parting tool flat on the rest, and then gently touch the turning with the point. Cut just deep enough to leave a shallow groove—about 1/16".

3. Now, burn in the grooves. Firmly tie each end of a 12" length of wire, such as single-strand picture-hanging wire, to a piece of dowel. With the lathe running, press the stretched wire into each groove.

4. Next, hollow out the bowl with your gouge. Before cutting the rabbet in the top, measure the lid. "They're all hand-cast lids. They can vary, and sometimes they aren't perfectly round," explains Darryl Nish of Craft Supplies USA. "Turners need to make the hole fit the lid they have."

5. Sand with progressively finer sandpaper, from 100- to 320-grit. Spray on three or four coats of lacquer, rubbing with 0000 steel wool between coats. Part from the lathe, and finish the bottom. Apply paste wax and buff.

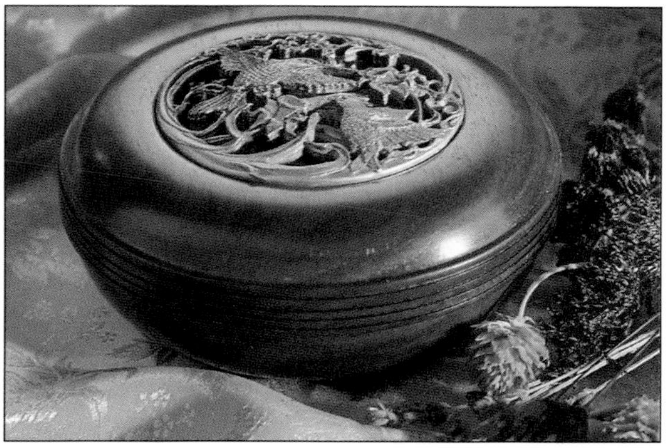

Buying Guide

• **Lid and potpourri.** Pewter hummingbird-design lid; 1 oz. potpourri. For current prices, contact Craft Supplies USA, 1287 E. 1120 S., Provo, UT 84601, or call 801-373-0917.

Supplies

Stock: Walnut bowl-turning blank, 3x6x6". Lathe tools: 3" faceplate with scrapwood auxiliary faceplate; ⅜" gouge, ¼" round-nose, ⅛" parting tool.

Lathe Speeds

Roughing: 600–900 rpm; finishing and sanding; 1,200–1,500 rpm.

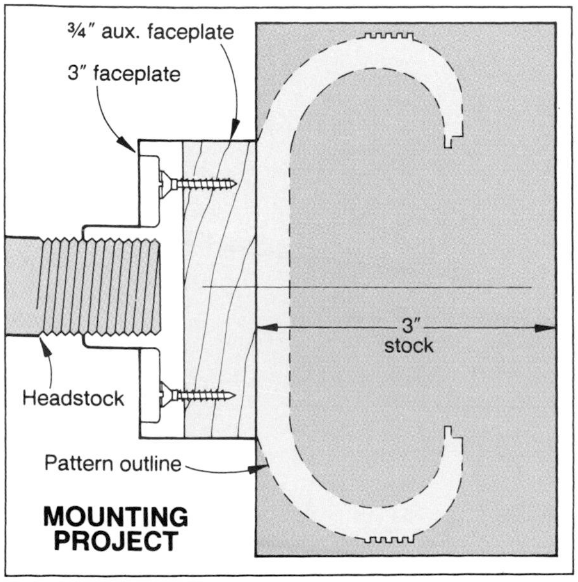
¾" aux. faceplate
3" faceplate
3"
stock
Headstock
Pattern outline
MOUNTING PROJECT

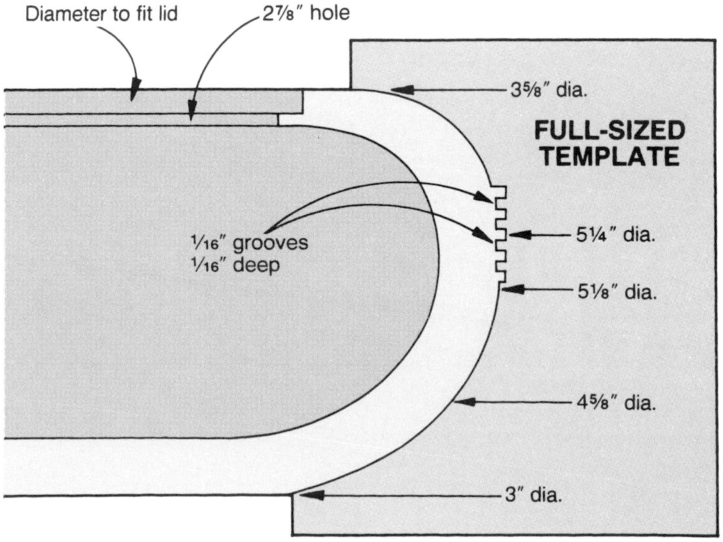
Diameter to fit lid
2⅞" hole
3⅝" dia.
FULL-SIZED TEMPLATE
1/16" grooves
1/16" deep
5¼" dia.
5⅛" dia.
4⅝" dia.
3" dia.

GALLERY-QUALITY QUILTED MAPLE BOWL

You'd expect to see a bowl of this quality in a gallery or similar showy setting. Truth is, you can proudly display this artistic creation in your home after just a few hours in the shop. And talk about a big return on your investment! We used less than $4 worth of wood for a bowl that looks like a million bucks.

Note: If you're new to wood-turning and/or stave construction, you'll want to refer to Basic Stave-Bowl Construction starting on page 30. *It will provide you with the necessary background information needed to successfully complete this project.*

Cutting the bowl wall parts to size

1. Cut a piece of 1⁄16"-thick stock (we chose maple) to 2×24" long for the center section (A). Cut another couple of strips the same length from scrap stock. (You'll use them later to test-cut staves.)

2. Now, cut the top and bottom walnut highlight strips (B) to ¼×1⁄16×24" long. Glue and clamp the maple piece between the two walnut strips where shown on the drawing *opposite*.

3. For the inset strips (C), cut a piece of ¾" stock to 1⅛×24" wide. Resaw it to ¼" thick, and cut eight 2½"-long pieces from the ¼" strip.

4. Tilt your saw blade 22½° from vertical center. Cut and dry-clamp eight test staves to check the fit of the joints. If they're not flush, adjust the blade angle, and repeat the process. Now, cut eight staves for the bowl ring (see the Bowl Ring Lamination drawing *opposite* for how these come out of the stave stock).

Gluing the staves

1. Cut two pieces of plywood 6" square each.

2. Dry-clamp the staves and inset strips to check the fit. Make any minor adjustments as suggested on *page 34* of the stave technique article. Glue and lightly clamp the pieces together as shown in the photo at *right*.

3. Position the ring between the two pieces of plywood, being sure to put waxed paper between the ring and plywood pieces. Clamp the assembly together as shown *opposite* to ensure flush tops and bottoms of the stave pieces. Tighten the clamp around the ring to pull the pieces firmly together.

4. Later, remove the clamp, and sand the top of the ring smooth. See *page 34* for how we do this.

Shaping the bowl

1. Center the staved ring over and glue it to a ¾" plywood auxiliary faceplate. Turn the outside

Apply an even coat of glue to the mating edges, place the assembly flat on waxed paper, and lightly clamp the bowl-wall segments together.

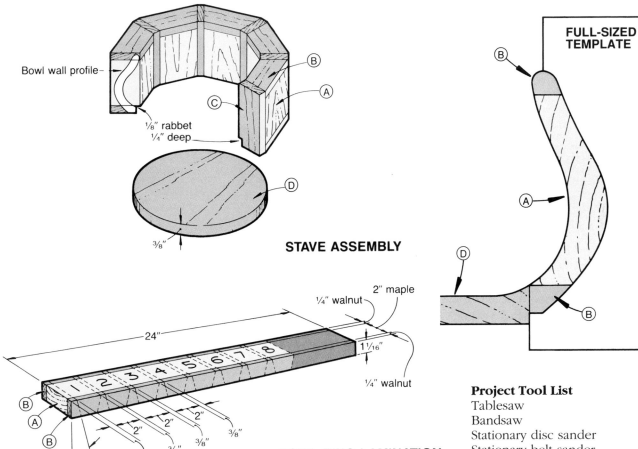

Bowl wall profile

⅛" rabbet
¼" deep

STAVE ASSEMBLY

⅜"

Ⓑ
Ⓐ
Ⓒ
Ⓓ

FULL-SIZED TEMPLATE

Ⓑ
Ⓐ
Ⓓ
Ⓑ

2" maple
¼" walnut

24"

1 1/16"

¼" walnut

Ⓑ
Ⓐ
Ⓑ

2"
2"
2"
⅜"
⅜"
⅜"
⅜"
⅜"

22½°

BOWL RING LAMINATION

Project Tool List
Tablesaw
Bandsaw
Stationary disc sander
Stationary belt sander
Drill press
  Sanding disc
Finishing sander
Lathe
  Faceplate
  Bowl gouge
  Side scraper
  Skew scraper
  Parting tool

Note: We built the project using the tools listed. You may be able to substitute other tools or equipment for listed items you don't have. Additional common hand tools and clamps may be required to complete the project.

Lightly clamp the staved ring between two pieces of plywood to hold the top and bottom edges flush. Then, firmly tighten the band clamps.

round, and true up the bottom of the ring. Next, turn a ⅛" rabbet ¼" deep for later housing the bottom. Remove the project from the lathe.

2. Lay out and bandsaw a ¾" walnut disk (D) ½" larger in diameter than the rabbeted opening. Center and mount the disk to an auxiliary faceplate. Turn the disk round; then, using a parting tool, turn it to ⅜" thick. Now, turn the disk to fit snugly into the rabbeted opening. Glue the disk into the rabbet.

3. Turn the bowl to shape. Refer to the template *above right* to reproduce the shape shown in the photo *opposite*. Apply the finish.

STACK 'EM UP LAMINATED BOWL

Very often in woodworking, it's the little touches that set apart certain projects from the rest. Here, we laminated squares of cardinal wood and oak veneer to make this simple bowl, one that will stand out no matter where you display it. For more information about faceplate turning technique, see the article beginning on *page 40.*

Forming the stack lamination

1. Cut three pieces of ¾" cardinal wood and two pieces of oak veneer to 7¼ x 7¼".

2. Stack the pieces as shown in the drawing at *right* (be sure to alternate the grain of the three cardinal wood pieces). Spread a thin, even coat of glue on all mating surfaces (we used a playing card to spread the glue out). With the edges of the pieces flush, clamp them together with several handscrews. Wait for the glue to dry and remove the handscrews.

3. Draw diagonals from corner to corner to find its center using a compass, mark 3⅝" radius on the lamination, and cut the piece to shape with a bandsaw, cutting on the *outside* of the marked circle

Mounting the work onto the lathe

1. Screw a piece of scrap ¾" plywood that's at least 6" square to your faceplate. Now, using another scrap piece of wood cut to the correct size, scribe the circumference (4¾") of the finished bowl base on the headstock side of the plywood (refer to Photo B and the

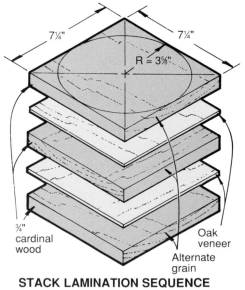

STACK LAMINATION SEQUENCE

FULL-SIZED TEMPLATE

90°

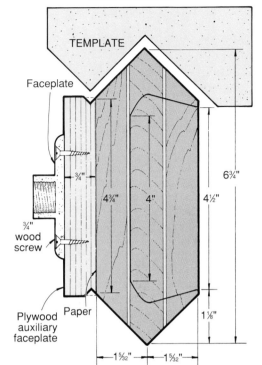

SIDE SECTION

TEMPLATE

Faceplate

Plywood auxiliary faceplate

Paper

¾" wood screw

¾"
4¾"
4"
6¾"
4½"
1⅛"
1⁵⁄₃₂" 1⁵⁄₃₂"

description on *page 40* of the techniques article for details about how to do this).

2. Unscrew the plywood faceplate from the headstock. Cut around the marked perimeter of the plywood. Mount the faceplate assembly back to your lathe.

3. Spread an even coat of glue on the exposed face of the plywood mounted on the faceplate. Quickly place a piece of paper on it. Now, before the glue sets, spread another even coat of glue on the exposed face of the paper. Position the tailstock center against the marked center on the top face of the lamination. Then, slide the tailstock/lamination firmly against the faceplate assembly. Lock the tailstock to the lathe bed; then tighten the tailstock spindle to "clamp" the lamination against the faceplate. Let the glue dry overnight.

First the outside, then the inside

1. Position the tool rest slightly above center and along the outside edge of the laminated blank. Set the lathe at a slow speed (400–600 rpm), use a spindle gouge to remove any "out-of-round" stock. Once you round-down the lamination, vibration will decrease and you can speed up to 800–1,000 rpm and reposition the tool rest.

2. Place a piece of carbon paper and a piece of cardboard under the full-sized template drawing accompanying the Side Section drawing *right*. Trace the shape of the template onto the cardboard. Now, cut the template to shape. Shape the outside of the bowl with a skew, stopping periodically to check the shape with the template.

3. To turn the inside, reposition the tool rest across the front of the bowl. Using a bowl gouge, clean out the inside of the bowl, being careful not to make the wall too thin at the top edge. Also make sure you don't cut through the bottom oak veneer layer. (We made extremely shallow cuts when we got close to the oak veneer to ensure that we wouldn't cut through it.)

Sanding and finishing the bowl

1. Remove the tool rest, and sand the inside and outside surfaces. (We wrapped sandpaper around a piece of felt and kept moving the sandpaper to prevent burning both the bowl and our fingers. We started with 100-grit, progressed through 150–220 grit and finally 320-grit sandpaper using a lathe speed of about 1,000 rpm).

2. Using a chisel and a mallet, work your way around the perimeter of the bowl, tapping gently at the paper line to wedge the bowl away from the plywood.

(We positioned the flat edge of the chisel against the bowl's bottom to prevent denting the cardinal wood.) Be careful not to mar the cardinal wood by driving the chisel too far in, or rocking the chisel back and forth to remove it. The laminated bowl should break cleanly from the plywood at the paper line.

3. Sand the bowl bottom smooth, being careful to keep it perfectly flat (we used a stationary belt sander for this operation). Apply the finish.

Project Tool List
Tablesaw
Bandsaw
Stationary belt sander
Lathe
    Faceplate
    ½" spindle gouge
    1" skew chisel
    ⅜" bowl gouge

Note: *We built the project using the tools listed. You may be able to substitute other tools or equipment for listed items you don't have. Additional common hand tools and clamps may be required to complete the project.*

DANDY SASSAFRAS FRUIT BOWL

Distinctively patterned sides put stave bowls in a class all their own. Not being satisfied with just a stunning bowl wall, we decided to go one step further and create an equally attractive bottom for our 9"-diameter fruit bowl.

Note: For more detailed information about how to plan, cut, assemble, and turn stave bowls, please read "Basic Stave-Bowl Construction" starting on page 30. Here we focus primarily on creating the sunburst bowl bottom.

Also, you'll need at least a 6" swing to turn this project on your lathe.

Cut, laminate, and form the staved bowl wall

1. Cut a piece of 1⅛"-thick stock (we used sassafras) to 3×30" long for the stave stock. See *page 32* for how to lay out and cut this piece. Also note in the Stave Stock drawing *opposite* how the identical grain pattern

of each stave segment relates to the grain direction of the stave stock.

2. Tilt your table-saw blade 15° from center, and bevel-rip both edges of the strip for a 2⅜" finished width. Straighten the blade.

3. Crosscut 12 staves 2" long for the bowl wall segments (A).

4. Dry-clamp the staves together to check the fit, and sand if necessary for tight joints as explained on *page 34*. Glue and clamp the pieces together to form the staved ring. Later, sand one end of the ring smooth, and glue it, centered, on a ¾" plywood auxiliary faceplate. Turn the outside of the bowl round, true up the bottom of the bowl wall, and turn a ⅛" rabbet ¼" deep into the inside edge of the wall.

Here's how to cut the bowl bottom pieces

1. Cut a piece of stock to 5½×32". Plane the stock to ½" thick, and cut 12 pieces of ¾"-thick stock to 2⅜×4⅞" for the bottom segments

(B). Draw layout lines on one of the pieces where shown on the drawing *opposite*.

2. Cut two pieces of ¾" particleboard to 4×12". Now, follow the three-step drawing *opposite* to form jig 1 and to cut one edge of each bottom segment. Follow Steps 4 and 5 on the drawing to form jig 2 and to cut the opposite edge of each segment to shape.

Gluing up the bottom

1. After forming a right angle with two wood strips, nail the strips to a piece of flat stock to form a jig as shown in the photo *opposite*.

2. Apply glue (we used regular woodworker's glue) to the mating edges of three of the bottom pieces, and "clamp" them as shown in the photo *opposite*. (We placed waxed paper between the bottom pieces and plywood to prevent them from sticking to each other.) Repeat for each of the remaining quarter sections. After the glue dries, check

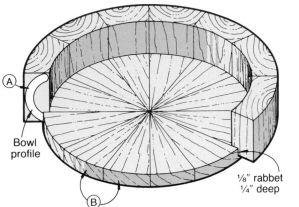

STAVE ASSEMBLY

(A)

Bowl profile

(B)

⅛" rabbet
¼" deep

BOTTOM SEGMENT LAYOUT BLOCK

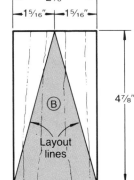

2⅝"

1⁵⁄₁₆" 1⁵⁄₁₆"

(B)

4⅞"

Layout lines

STAVE STOCK

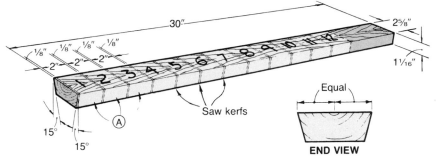

30"

⅛" ⅛" ⅛" ⅛"

2" 2" 2"

2⅝"

1¹⁄₁₆"

15°

15°

(A)

Saw kerfs

Equal

END VIEW

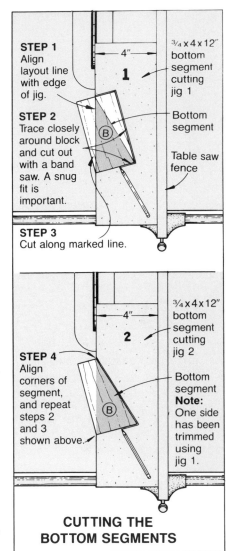

STEP 1
Align layout line with edge of jig.

STEP 2
Trace closely around block and cut out with a band saw. A snug fit is important.

STEP 3
Cut along marked line.

STEP 4
Align corners of segment, and repeat steps 2 and 3 shown above.

¾ x 4 x 12" bottom segment cutting jig 1

4"

1

(B)

Bottom segment

Table saw fence

¾ x 4 x 12" bottom segment cutting jig 2

4"

2

(B)

Bottom segment
Note: One side has been trimmed using jig 1.

CUTTING THE BOTTOM SEGMENTS

"Clamp" three bottom segments together by nailing them into a square corner.

each quarter section for square, and sand square if necessary.

3. Glue and "clamp" two of the quarter sections together to form a half section. Repeat to form the other half section.

4. Now, glue and band-clamp the two half sections together, keeping the points in the center aligned.

Turning the bowl

1. Carefully center and mount the laminated bottom to an auxiliary faceplate, and turn it to a ⅜" thickness. Now, reduce the base diameter until the base fits snugly into the rabbet in the bottom of the bowl wall. Glue the bottom into the

rabbet, aligning its joint lines with those of the bowl wall. Later, finish turning the bowl to shape using the full-size template shown at *right* as a guide. Sand smooth, apply the finish, and part from the auxiliary faceplate.

Project Tool List

Tablesaw
Bandsaw
Stationary disc sander
Stationary belt sander
Drill press
    Sanding disc
Finishing sander
Lathe
    Faceplate
    Bowl gouge
    Side scraper
    Skew scraper
    Parting tool

Note: *We built the project using the tools listed. You may be able to substitute other tools or equipment for listed items you don't have. Additional common hand tools and clamps may be required to complete the project.*

FULL-SIZED TEMPLATE

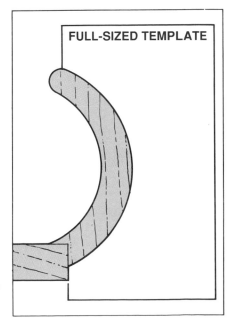

CLASSY COVERED CANDY CADDY

We know one thing for sure about this project—it's a lot easier to turn than it is to pronounce. Made from Honduras mahogany, which we vouch for as a wonderful turning wood, this container with lid has enough design elements to make it interesting, and it's useful to boot. For more information about the basics of faceplate turning, see *page 40*.

Preparing the stock

1. Crosscut a piece of 4x4" mahogany stock to 6" long. Draw diagonal lines on one end to locate the center.

2. Carefully center and mount the marked end of the stock to the faceplate. (We used #10x1" brass flathead wood screws.)

3. Slide the tailstock to the other end of the mahogany stock, and lock it in position. The tailstock helps support the workpiece and reduces vibration when you round-down the square stock.

Let's start turning!

1. With the lathe running at a low speed (400–600 rpm), round-down the mahogany square stock with a spindle gouge.

2. Using the Container Layout drawing as a guide, lay out the location of the top and bottom points of the container and lid on your workpiece. Make shallow parting cuts at each of these points.

3. Use carbon paper to transfer the full-sized lid template (shown *opposite*) to a piece of cardboard. Cut the cardboard template to shape. Now, increase the lathe speed to 800–1,000 rpm, and use a small skew chisel, gouge, and parting tool to form the lid and finial. After shaping the lid, slide the tailstock away.

4. Sand the lid exterior smooth. Then, with the lathe speed at about 500 rpm and using a parting tool as shown in the photo *opposite,* cut the lid apart from the workpiece. Be sure to keep one hand below the lid so you can catch it as it falls free.

Note: We caught ours in the right hand to prevent the lid from spinning off the lathe and getting marred or dented.

Turning the container

1. Again using the Container Layout drawing as a guide, and a parting tool, cut away all excess material from the top of the container. Then, hollow out the inside of the container, being careful not to go too deep or get the wall thickness too thin. Continually check the fit of the lid against the opening of the container, and turn the opening to within 1⁄16" of the diameter of the lid's lip. Then, sand the opening until the lid fits (but lifts easily from) the container. After turning several containers with lids,

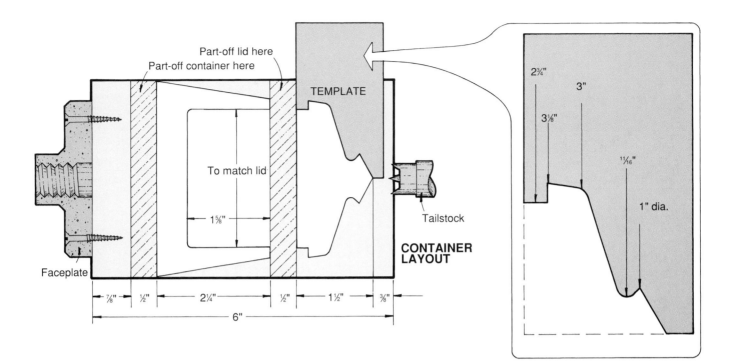

Part-off lid here
Part-off container here

TEMPLATE

To match lid

1⅝"

Faceplate

Tailstock

CONTAINER LAYOUT

⅞" ½" 2¼" ½" 1½" ⅜"

6"

2¾"
3"
3⅛"
1¹¹⁄₁₆"
1" dia.

FULL-SIZED TEMPLATE

you will get such a perfect fit that you can hear and feel a slight vacuum when pulling the lid off.

2. Turn the outside of the container to shape so that the taper of its sidewalls matches that of the lid.

3. Sand the outside of the container smooth at about 1,000 rpm. Turn the lathe off and do the final sanding *with the grain.*

4. Reduce the lathe speed to the 500 rpm range, and use a parting

tool to separate the container from the remaining portion of the mahogany. Finally, sand the bottom of the container smooth and flat to avoid rocking (we sanded ours on a stationary belt sander).

5. Use a tack rag to wipe off any sawdust, and spray or brush on a clear finish. (With the lathe running, we sprayed on several light coats of lacquer, steel-wooling between coats with 0000 steel wool.)

Buying Guide
• **Mahogany turning square.**
4x4x12". For current prices, contact Constantine's, 2050 Eastchester Rd., Bronx, NY 10461, or call 800-223-8087.

Project Tool List
Lathe
    Faceplate
    Revolving tail center
    ½" skew chisel
    ⅜", ½" spindle gouges
    ⅜" bowl gouge
    Parting tool
Stationary belt sander

Note: We built the project using the tools listed. You may be able to substitute other tools or equipment for listed items you don't have. Additional common hand tools and clamps may be required to complete the project.

TERRIFIC TURNED TRIO

What happens to the stock inside of most turning projects? Chips, shavings, and more chips. But this efficient project wastes little. And better yet, even a novice woodworker can easily turn our cherry-and-walnut lamination into three handsome bowls.

Prepare the thin stock for laminating

1. To form the 11¼"-square walnut (A) and cherry layers (B) shown in the Bowl Lamination drawing *opposite bottom,* rip and crosscut one piece of ¾"-thick walnut to 3¾" wide by 70" long (or if you prefer, two 35"-long pieces). Rip and crosscut one piece of ¾"-thick cherry to 3¾" wide by 36" long.

2. Resaw the cherry board to obtain two ¼"-thick pieces measuring 3¾×36". (The two-step Resaw Setup drawing *opposite* shows how we resawed two ¼"-thick slabs from the ¾"-thick cherry stock.) Plane or resaw the walnut to ½" thick. (To resaw the ¾"-thick walnut, we set the fence ½" from the inside edge of the blade.)

RESAW SETUP

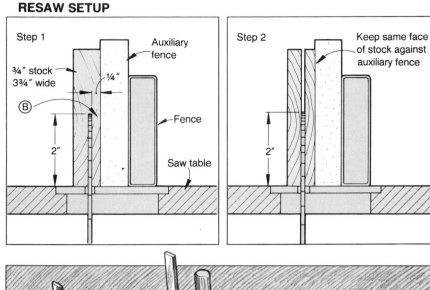

Step 1

¾" stock
3¾" wide

B

¼"

2"

Auxiliary fence

Fence

Saw table

Step 2

Keep same face of stock against auxiliary fence

2"

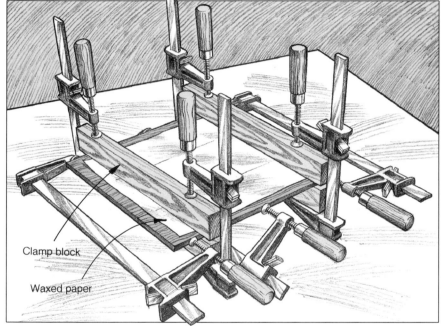

Clamp block

Waxed paper

BOWL LAMINATION

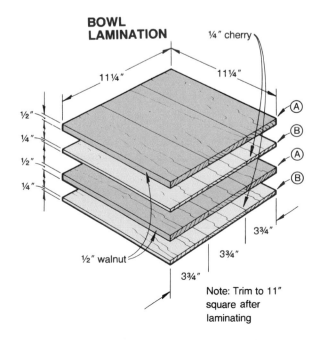

11¼"

11¼"

¼" cherry

½"

¼"

½"

¼"

A

B

A

B

3¾"

3¾"

3¾"

½" walnut

Note: Trim to 11" square after laminating

Bill of Materials

Part	Finished Size*			Mat.	Qty.
	T	W	L		
A* 1st & 3rd layers	½"	11"	11"	W	2
B* 2nd & 4th layers	¼"	11"	11"	C	2
C* base	¾"	10¾" dia.		W	1
D* base	¾"	8¾" dia.		W	1
E* base	¾"	6¾" dia.		W	1

*Initially cut parts marked with an * oversized as directed in the instructions. Then, trim or turn each to the finished size.

Material Key: W–walnut, C–cherry.

3. Crosscut six 11¼"-long pieces from the walnut stock and six 11¼"-long pieces from the cherry. From ¾" stock, cut four clamp blocks to 1" wide by 12" long.

4. Spread yellow woodworker's glue on the mating edges of three ¼" cherry pieces (enough for one layer). Clamp these three pieces edge to edge as shown at *left.* Let glue dry overnight. Later, remove the clamps, clamp blocks, and waxed paper. Carefully scrape off the excess glue. Sand both lamination faces smooth, being careful not to round over the outside edges or sand a depression at the joint lines. Now, form the other three lamination layers the same way.

Now, ready the bowl blanks for turning

1. First, stack the four pieces in the configuration shown on the Bowl Lamination drawing at *left.* Next, spread a uniform coat of glue on the mating faces of the four layers and restack the pieces in the same order. (We used an old credit card to spread the glue evenly.)

2. Clamp the lamination, aligning the edges and ends. (As shown in the Edge Joining drawing, we used the same clamp blocks to distribute the clamping pressure and to avoid marring the top and bottom pieces with the clamp heads.) Let the lamination set overnight.

3. Remove the clamps, clamp blocks, and waxed paper. Now, trim the lamination to 11" square.

continued

TERRIFIC TURNED TRIO
continued

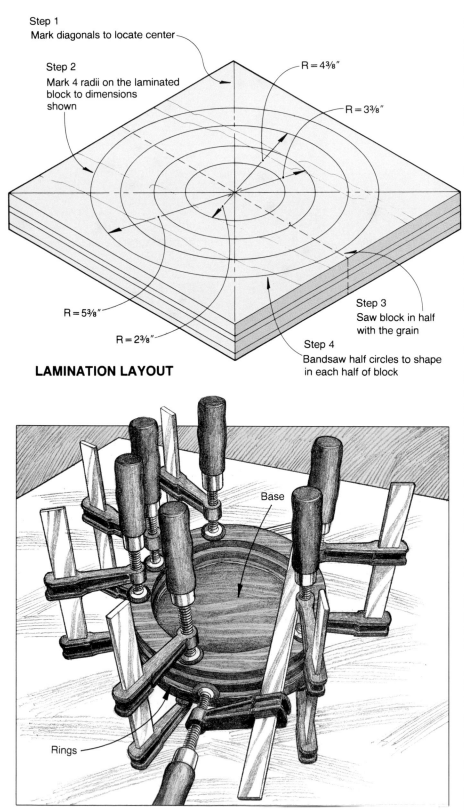

Step 1
Mark diagonals to locate center

Step 2
Mark 4 radii on the laminated block to dimensions shown

R = 4⅜″

R = 3⅜″

R = 5⅜″

R = 2⅜″

Step 3
Saw block in half with the grain

Step 4
Bandsaw half circles to shape in each half of block

LAMINATION LAYOUT

Base

Rings

4. Following the four steps on the Lamination Layout drawing at *left,* scribe the four bowl radii. Next, cut the block in half (with the grain). Now, bandsaw the six half rings to shape, cutting on the lines.

5. To form the ¾"-thick walnut bowl bases, edge-join stock for one 11" square, one 9" square, and one 7" square.

6. Hold the largest half rings together tightly, and mark their circumference on the 11"-square walnut base. Repeat this procedure for the other two bowl bases.

7. Bandsaw the walnut bases to shape. Now, glue and clamp the half rings together and to their mating walnut bases as shown in the drawing *below left.*

Have fun turning your nesting bowls

1. To make the auxiliary faceplates, scribe a 6", 8", and 10" circle on pieces of 1"-thick stock. (We planed down a 2x12 so we would have plenty of thickness later when parting the bowl from the faceplate. If you use a thinner auxiliary faceplate, you might accidentally strike the mounting screws with the parting tool when separating the bowl from the faceplate.)

2. Bandsaw the three auxiliary faceplates to shape. Glue the faceplates to the walnut bases.

3. Carefully center and screw a 3" faceplate to the auxiliary face-plate for the smallest bowl. See the Shaping the Bowl drawing *opposite* for additional details.

4. Thread this assembly onto your lathe headstock spindle. Using a speed of about 750 rpm, true up the outside bowl surface and faceplate to 6". (We used a ½" gouge. Although a scraper would work, we prefer a sharp gouge and a cutting action to minimize tearout of the end grain.) Turn the bowl base to shape as shown *opposite.*

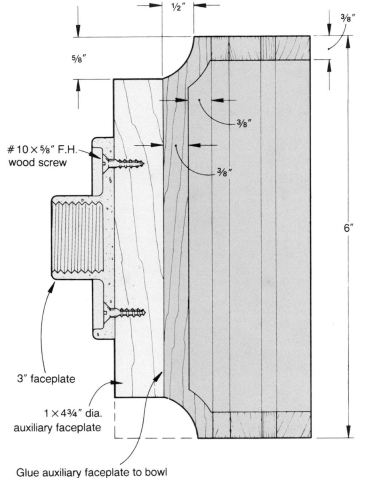

½"

⅝"

3/8"

3/8"

3/8"

10 × ⅝" F.H.
wood screw

6"

3" faceplate

1 × 4¾" dia.
auxiliary faceplate

Glue auxiliary faceplate to bowl

SHAPING THE BOWL

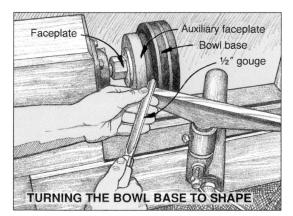

Faceplate

Auxiliary faceplate

Bowl base

½" gouge

TURNING THE BOWL BASE TO SHAPE

5. Increase the lathe speed to 1,000 or 1,250 rpm, and hand-sand the bowl exterior smooth with 80-, 100-, and 150-grit sandpaper.

6. To turn the inside of the bowl to shape, reposition the tool rest, decrease the speed to 750 rpm, and reduce the wall thickness to ⅜". (Again, we used a ½" gouge.)

7. With a parting tool or ¼" gouge, turn the contoured corners of the bowl-bottom interior to the shape shown on the Shaping the Bowl drawing. Next, turn the bowl's bottom to ⅜" thick. Be careful you don't cut the bottom too thin or cut through the bowl base. Now, increase the speed and hand-sand the bowl interior.

You're now ready to apply the finish

1. Finish-sand the entire bowl (we used 220-grit paper). With the bowl still mounted on the lathe, apply the finish to the bowl (we brushed on Behlen's Salad Bowl Finish). After the finish has dried, start the lathe and lightly buff the finish with 0000 steel wool. Do not buff through the finish. Apply a second and third coat, buffing lightly between coats with steel wool.

2. Using a parting tool, cut through the auxiliary faceplate (next to the walnut base) and separate the base from the auxiliary faceplate. When making the parting cut, angle the tool about 3–5° to the right of center to create a slightly concave base. This will prevent the finished bowl from rocking when sitting on a flat surface.

3. Sand the base smooth, sign and date it, and then apply the same finishing material to it.

4. Now, repeat these processes with the two larger bowls using your 6" metal faceplate.

Buying Guide
• **Behlen's Salad Bowl Finish.** One pint, Catalog No. 85006. For current price, contact Armor Products, Box 445, East Northport, NY 11731, or call 516-462-6228.

Project Tool List
Tablesaw
Bandsaw
Lathe
    Faceplate
    ½" bowl gouge
    Parting tool

Note: We built the project using the tools listed. You may be able to substitute other tools or equipment for listed items you don't have. Additional common hand tools and clamps may be required to complete the project.

ACKNOWLEDGMENTS

Writers

Larry Clayton—Basic Stave-Bowl Construction, pages 30–35; Faceplate Turning, pages 40–45

Larry Johnston with Gary Zeff and Todd Hoyer, pages 17–19

Bill Krier—How to Sharpen Turning and Carving Tools, pages 11–15

Bill Krier with James R. Downing—Stack-Laminated Bowls, pages 50–55

Peter J. Stephano with Walt Panek—Dry Green Bowls in Minutes, pages 20–23

Project Designers

Walt Becker—Turned Rolling Pin and Storage Rack, pages 66–68

Mark Burhans—Candle Holders with a Flare, page 65

James Downing—Turned Mortar and Pestle, pages 71–73; Southwest-Inspired Bowl, pages 79–82; Gallery-Quality Quilted Maple Bowl, pages 84–85; Stack 'em Up Laminated Bowl, pages 86–87; Dandy Sassafras Fruit Bowl, pages 88–89; Classy Covered Candy Caddy, pages 90–91; Terrific Turned Trio, pages 92–95

C. L. Gatzke—Masterpiece Music Box, pages 57–58; Pewter-Topped Potpourri Bowl, page 83

Dave Hout—Construct-A-Chuck, pages 6–7; Lathe-Laid Eggs, pages 74–75

Lanny Lyell—Turning Jig for Better Bottoms, page 5

Ron Odegaard—Spirited Foursome of Yuletide Turnings, pages 76–77

S. Gary Roberts, Turn Scraps into Pincushions, page 59

C. Robert Taylor—Split-Turned Vase, pages 62–64

Warren Vienneau—Decorator Oil Lamps, pages 60–61

Photographers

Craig Anderson
Brian Blauser
Bob Calmer
Gordon Diffendaffer
Jeff Frey
Jim Hale
John Hetherington
Hopkins Associates
William Hopkins
Jim Kascoutas
Peter Mettler
Dan Olmstad
J.R. Raybourn
David Schwefel
Gary Zeff

Illustrators

Jamie Downing
Kim Downing
Mike Henry
Todd Hoyer
Carson Ode
Greg Roberts
Jim Stevenson
Bill Zaun

If you would like to order any additional copies of our books, call 1-800-678-2803 or check with your local bookstore.
